GRAMMAR & STYLE

GRAMMAR & STYLE

for examination candidates and others

Michael Dummett

Wykeham Professor of Logic Emeritus
in the University of Oxford

Duckworth

Second impression July 1993
First published in June 1993 by
Gerald Duckworth & Co. Ltd.
The Old Piano Factory
48 Hoxton Square, London N1 6PB
Tel: 071 729 5986
Fax: 071 729 0015

A catalogue record for this book is available
from the British Library

ISBN 0 7156 2422 9

Typeset by Ray Davies
Printed in Great Britain by
Redwood Books, Trowbridge

Contents

To Andy and Paul

Preface

This little book is intended primarily to help University examination candidates – those taking Finals examinations for the BA, writers of theses for Master's degrees or doctorates, and those sitting other examinations – to write grammatically correct and stylistically inoffensive sentences. It will, I hope, also be of help to others (for instance anyone uncertain when to use **its** and when **it's**).

I was prompted to compose it by the experience of being an examiner for one of the Finals examinations at Oxford. Many of the mistakes noted here were committed by a large number – in some cases, by most – of the candidates whose scripts I read, and many of the unattributed examples are taken or adapted from them. I do not wish, however, to suggest that candidates for university degrees are uniquely liable to make such mistakes. Other errors I have listed here I have met with in television news broadcasts; others again in communications from the General Board of Oxford University.

Since I ceased to be an examiner, I had to find another source from which to draw examples of erroneous grammar, style and spelling. I found it in casual reading, particularly of the quality Press. No suggestion is intended that the newspapers from which I have quoted are worse in this respect than others; examples are so frequent that I have not needed to search them out in what I should not ordinarily read. I believe, however, that newspaper editors and journalists bear a heavy responsibility for the prevalence of faulty spelling and grammar. Students who have not been trained to be conscious of how words are spelled and sentences constructed naturally absorb mistakes they come across in their reading. Those whose trade is in the printed word have a duty to the language, over whose use they have an exceptional influence.

To avoid excessive use of quotation marks, bold type is used for words, phrases and sentences quoted or referred to. I have concentrated on uses of particular words and on how words are put together; there is only a short section on spelling.

Frequent comparisons have been made with other languages. Of some of these I have no more than a smattering; the value of knowing the rudiments of foreign languages, with no ambition to learn them properly, is seldom remarked. The particular character of each language is given it by the word order, grammatical constructions and modes of expression peculiar to it. By becoming aware of the different possibilities realised in various languages, we become more conscious of the features that give *our* language its special character, and hence more careful to preserve them.

Some readers, having glanced through this book, may scorn it because they would not think of making most of the mistakes they have seen listed. It may well be of use to them, all the same: even if there are only one or two items telling them something they did not know or had not noticed, that will surely be worth the time taken to read it through. Others may light on turns of phrase they frequently use but I have condemned. They should not put the book aside in disgust, resentment or indignation; I may be right, and they wrong. We are none of us infallible, as a tactless cardinal once remarked to Pius IX; anyone who is sceptical of any of my rulings should check with a dictionary or with someone whose command of English he trusts.

It *is* annoying to be criticised for one's English style, as I know very well; the first article I submitted for publication in an academic journal was rejected by the editor on grounds of style, and the first book I wrote was accepted by the Oxford University Press on condition that I improve it stylistically. I have myself made, in print, some of the errors that I here stigmatise as such; and I offer no guarantee that the prose of this book is free of errors, though I have striven to make it so.

We all have a responsibility, however, to the language we use in speech and writing; especially in writing, because it stands as an example, good or bad, to others after us. Our language, like other languages, is a subtle instrument, and all its users must wish to improve the way they employ it. That can be done only through understanding better how it works; and so we should always have the humility to accept correction of our use of it.

There is also a general source of resistance to the very idea that there can be such a thing as a misspelled word, a grammatical mistake or a word used in the wrong sense. A common slogan is 'You can't stop the language from changing'. It is true enough that one should not even want the language not to change; but it is *we* who change it, and it is up to us how fast it changes and whether it changes for the worse or for the better. In a literate community, like our own, the language does not comprise only the words spoken in conversation or printed in newspapers: it consists also in the writings of past centuries. An effect of rapid change is that what was written only a short time ago becomes difficult to understand; such a change is of itself destructive. It cannot be helped that Chaucer presents some obstacles to present-day readers; but I have been told that philosophy students nowadays have trouble understanding the English of Hume and Berkeley, and even, sometimes, of nineteenth-century writers. That is pure loss, and a sure sign that some people's use of English is changing much *too* fast.

Although a few spelling mistakes, like **presumptious**, arise from mispronunciations, spelling is obviously a feature of the written language alone. English, is, so far as I know, unique among languages written with a phonetic script in that its spelling must be learned word by word, and cannot be deduced from a few simple rules. This, though a light price to pay for not having to memorise genders or complicated inflections, is a regrettable burden on anyone learning English, whether as a first or a second language; but the process has now gone so far that it could be reversed only at the cost of making everything printed before the reform unreadable. We are stuck with a situation in which correct spelling is something everyone is required to know, on pain of being thought badly educated (or, sometimes, of being misunderstood).

As for grammar, the view that it does not matter is not thought out. Suppose that you bought a 'Teach Yourself' book for a language you wanted to learn, and it said that all there was to learning it was to acquire the vocabulary: the language had no grammar. Obviously, that would not be possible: there could not be a language with no principles about how to put the words together. We cannot do without grammar: we can only exchange existing grammatical rules for new ones. That, of course, is fine if the new rules improve the expressive power of the language, and bad if they impoverish it: but, before we promote new rules, we shall do well to make sure we know what the existing ones are.

PRELIMINARY TEST

Before reading further, you may find it instructive to see how many mistakes you can spot in the following text.

Neither capitalism nor socialism are capable of diffusing this problem; and neither is it desireable that either solution is

attempted. We should not loose this opportunity to not only devise a new type of system but to at the same time manage our affairs such that we remain within the broad parameters defined by our democratic tradition. Having said this, it is important to take on board the fact that unequivocably disasterous consequences will result from us trying to run before we can walk. Those sort of consequences have already lead to unrest and conflict in the majority of the continent; we can only escape them if we forego our habitual inclination to act in haste and repent at leasure. The above quote from the German Chancellor, and it's stern words of warning, exemplifies some of the best thinking about these matters that are taking place at this moment in time; that is why it has had such positive feedback. We ought to better appreciate that opportunities seldom present themselves other than briefly to whomever can take advantage of them; for he who would not be left adrift in the ongoing march of events, there is no other alternative but to seek a middle path between one calamity laden socio-economic mechanism and the other. We must put to ourselves the question as to whether to seek it, or, alternately, to ever sink deeper into stagnation in terms of our economy.

Do not attempt to rewrite the paragraph: it has very little meaning.

Warning

A hasty reader might wrongly conclude from the attributed examples in what follows that those to the left of centre write poorer English than those on the right. The correct conclusion is that I am more likely to read them.

1. Parts of Speech

It is impossible to set out grammatical principles succinctly without using the terminology that serves to distinguish what were traditionally known as 'parts of speech' – the various categories to which different words belong: noun, adjective, verb, etc. By using these terms, a rule can often be *stated* briefly when, without them, much verbiage would be required; in other cases, the reason for a rule can be *explained* by their means. Conversely, however, the distinctions between the various categories cannot be accurately drawn without expounding some grammar. This is because they are *grammatical* categories. The conventional way of explaining them tries to distinguish them according to the kind of senses borne by words in different categories, saying, for example, that a verb is a 'doing word'. The attempt must fail, because it is not the *sense* of a word, but its *role* in sentences, that determines to which category it belongs. The verb **resemble** and the adjective **similar** have exactly the same sense: to say that Princeton and Cambridge are similar is the same as to say that they resemble one another. The *only* difference between the uses of these words is that **resemble** is a verb, so that it would be a mistake to say **Princeton is resemble to Cambridge**, while **similar** is an adjective, and hence it would be an equal mistake to say **Princeton similars Cambridge**.

Readers who feel perfectly happy that they know the difference between a preposition and a conjunction, or an adverb and an adjective, may skip this preliminary section and go straight to Section 2. Any who are at all unsure will do better to stick with it, since the differences will play an important part in what follows. They will not be wasting their time, because even this section contains a certain amount of grammar, for the reason just explained.

(a) VERBS

There is a thin truth to the dictum that verbs are 'doing words', in that **do** or **does** may stand proxy for a verb or verb-phrase. I may say **Princeton resembles Cambridge more than it does Oxford**; and here **does** stands proxy for **resembles**, just as **it** stands proxy for **Princeton**. You may reply **Harvard does, too**; and this time **does** stands proxy for the whole phrase **resembles Cambridge more than it does Oxford**. But the verb **to do**, in these sentences, is as empty of content as the word **thing** in **That was a brave thing to say**; there is no suggestion that resembling is any kind of act, or resembling Cambridge more than Oxford any kind of activity. One could not sensibly say **What he said was brave, all right, but I should hardly call it a thing**: the speaker was not guilty of the alleged fallacy of reification, but used **thing** as a dummy noun because grammar demanded a noun in that place, while the thought he was expressing supplied none. The impersonal use of the pronoun **it** is a similar phenomenon: one could not reply to the statement **It's raining** by saying **Something's raining, indeed, but I doubt whether *it* is**, since **it** here serves only to supply a subject for the verb when English grammar requires one.

The German for 'verb' is **Zeitwort**, literally 'time-word'; and this indicates the best way to identify verbs. In their most common uses, they have *tenses*, to indicate whether the speaker is talking about something as happening or being the case now, or as having happened or been the case in the past, or as going to happen or be the case in the future. Tenses are formed in two ways. One is by inflecting (changing the form of) the verb, as the present-tense forms **is, brings, steals, walks, points** are changed to the past-tense forms **was, brought, stole, walked, pointed**. The other, extremely common in English, is by the use of an auxiliary verb like **has, is** and **will**. Thus the future-tense forms are **will be, will bring, will walk, will steal** and **will point**; and the perfect tense – a form of past tense used to indicate a present condition resulting from a past action or state of affairs – is formed by **has**: **has been, has brought, has stolen, has walked, has pointed**. The auxiliary **is** is used to form the continuous present tense, indicating something currently in progress: **is being, is bringing, is stealing, is walking, is pointing**. Different forms of the principal verb are used after these three auxiliaries: **be** and **bring** in **will be** and **will bring** are *infinitives*; **being** and **bringing** in **is being** and **is bringing** are *present participles*; and **been** and **brought** in **has been** and **has brought** are *past participles*.

In Italian, the same word **tempo** is used for 'tense' and 'time'. In English, the two do not always match exactly: for instance, **I am meeting him tomorrow** uses the present tense to speak of a future event.

Of course, verbs are also inflected for person and for number (singular or plural): **is** becomes **am** after **I**, and **are** after **they**; **brings** becomes **bring** after **I** or **they**.

These simple grammatical facts are doubtless well known to almost every reader: they are mentioned here only as affording the simplest way to identify a word as being a verb. More will be said about verbs in Section 2, for instance about the distinction between transitive and intransitive verbs; in this preliminary section, we are concerned only with how to recognise the different categories.

(b) ARTICLES

There are only two words in this category: the *definite article* **the**, and the *indefinite article* **a** or **an**. In many languages, but not in English, the indefinite article and the numerical adjective meaning 'one' are the same word; but, as in those languages, the indefinite article can be used in English only with a singular noun, the definite article with one in the singular or in the plural.

(c) THE SUBJECT

Being a *subject* is not an enduring trait of any word, like being an adverb; it is a role played within a particular sentence by a word or phrase, which may play a different role in other sentences. It is, however, hard to explain which words belong to the category of *nouns* without first explaining how to pick out the subject of a sentence, something it is in any case important to know.

In English, though not in every language, every sentence must contain a verb (we may count an auxiliary, taken together with the principal verb it is attached to, as forming a single verb). Occasionally, the verb may be 'understood' (tacitly supplied from the context), notably in the answer to a question: to the question **How many did you eat?**, the one-word answer **Five** is of course perfectly grammatical. Complex sentences are constructed out of two or more simple sentences, and then contain two or more verbs: **The assassins, whose hands were stained with Caesar's blood, looked down upon him where he lay** contains three verbs (**were stained, looked, lay**), and may be regarded as formed from the three simple sentences **The assassins looked down upon Caesar**, **The assassins' hands were stained with Caesar's blood** and **Caesar lay there**. The parts of the complex sentence corresponding to the simple sentences from which we can view it as having been formed are called *clauses*: a clause, like a simple sentence, must have a verb. The verb of a simple sentence or of a clause must be of *finite* form, that is, not an infinitive such as **to go**, a participle such as **going** and **gone**, or the like. In English, though again not in all languages, a finite verb must always have a *subject* (not 'understood' but explicit). How should the subject of a simple sentence or clause be picked out from the rest?

Usually, it is very easy: in the great majority of sentences, the subject stands at the beginning of the sentence and extends until the verb. The subject of **The assassins looked down upon Caesar** is **The assassins**; that of **The assassins' hands were stained with Caesar's blood** is **The assassins' hands**; and that of **Caesar lay there** is **Caesar**.

We may thus regard simple sentences as falling apart into the subject and the verb-phrase, the latter comprising everything but the subject. If we count a pronoun like **you** or **they**, or, again, like **everything**, as constituting a noun-phrase, the subject is always a noun-phrase, although not every noun-phrase is a subject; in **The assassins' hands were stained with Caesar's blood**, **Caesar's blood** is a noun-phrase, but it is not the subject of the sentence.

The rule that the subject consists of everything preceding the verb is very rough. In a complex sentence, a whole clause may intervene between the subject and the verb, as in **The assassins, when they had finished their fell work, looked down upon Caesar**: the subject of this sentence is still only **The assassins**. But in a simple sentence almost the only expression that can separate subject from verb is an adverb or adverbial phrase. Thus, in **The assassins furtively glanced at Caesar's corpse**, the subject remains **The assassins**: the adverb **furtively** is part of the verb-phrase. What is the reason for saying this? A noun-phrase always answers a 'Who ... ?' or 'What ... ?' question. Thus the answer to **Who was it the assassins looked down upon?** is **Caesar**, and the answer to **With what were the assassins' hands stained?** is **Caesar's blood**. But the subject gives the answer to a 'Who ... ?' or 'What ... ?' question when the gap is filled by the whole verb-phrase. **The assassins** is the answer to **Who glanced at Caesar's corpse?**; the answer **The assassins furtively** would be facetious or silly. Indeed, the proper question is **Who furtively glanced at Caesar's corpse?**; **furtively** qualifies **glanced**, and is therefore part of the verb-phrase, not of the subject.

Adverbs and adverbial phrases have great (though not total) licence in their placing: as well as intervening between the subject and the verb, they can stand at the beginning of a sentence. Examples are **Stealthily, he slid the drawer open, On the following day she bicycled to her cousin's house** and **Without a moment's hesitation, he signed both documents**. The adverb **Stealthily** and the adverbial phrases **On the following day** and **Without a moment's hesitation** can easily be seen not to be part of the subject from the fact that they could with equal naturalness be transferred to the end of these sentences. More difficult to classify is a parenthetical adjective like **undeterred** in **Undeterred, the candidate's wife rose to her feet** or **The candidate's wife, undeterred, rose to her feet. Undeterred** is not quite an adverb here, since it was the candidate's wife who was undeterred, rather than her rising to her feet; but it could not be placed in front of the principal noun **wife** in the subject – it would sound silly to say **The candidate's undeterred wife**. Something of the same occurs when there is a second noun-phrase in 'apposition' to the subject, offering a further description of the person or thing referred to, as in **The candidate's wife, by far the most beautiful woman in the room, rose to her feet**. It does not much matter whether we count the parenthetical adjective, or the phrase in apposition, as part of the subject or not: no serious ambiguity in the concept of the subject of a sentence results from leaving the point undecided.

The standard English word-order admits of inversion for rhetorical or poetic effect: in **All mimsy were the borogoves**, the subject is of course **the borogoves**. It should be obvious that the natural order is **The borogoves were all mimsy**; for, while one can ask **What were the borogoves?**, receiving the answer **All mimsy**, one cannot ask **What did you say were the borogoves?**, but only **What did you say the borogoves were? The borogoves** answers the appropriate question **What were all mimsy?** or **What did you say were all mimsy?** Inversion also occurs in questions: **The Greeks are bearing gifts** becomes **Are the Greeks bearing gifts?**, and as **the Greeks** is the subject of the one, so it is of the other. Certain words, such as **nor**, when they introduce a clause, demand an inversion, as in **Nor shall my sword sleep in my hand**; from the uninverted form, it is apparent that **my sword** is the subject of **shall sleep**.

It should now be clear how to identify the subject of a simple sentence or of a clause – at least of a clause forming a whole sentence preceded by a conjunction like **when** or **if**. A relative clause like **whose hands were stained with Caesar's blood** is signalled by the occurrence, at or near its beginning, by a relative pronoun like **who, whom, whose** or **which**. In the simple sentence from which the relative clause can be regarded as derived, there will be a noun-phrase in place of the relative pronoun; by deciding the subject of the simple sentence, we can decide that of the relative clause. The clause **whose hands were stained with Caesar's blood** is derived from, say, **Their hands were stained with Caesar's blood**, in which **Their hands** is the subject; so **whose hands** is the subject of the clause. But **whose hands he had clasped in friendship** is derived from **He had clasped their hands in friendship**, the subject of which is **He**; and so **he** is the subject of *this* clause.

(d) NOUN-PHRASES

If you can recognise the subject of a sentence, you can also identify a noun-phrase that is not the subject of the sentence in which it occurs; for a noun-phrase always could be the subject of another sentence. Thus in **Brutus plunged the sharpened dagger into Caesar's breast**, both **the sharpened dagger** and **Caesar's breast** are noun-phrases, though neither is the subject. We are allowing pronouns to count as noun-phrases, and they present a minor exception, since they inflect for case: that is to say, they change their form according to their role in the sentence. The first-person pronoun **I** has that form only when it is the subject, as in **I am glad to see you**, or follows the verb **to be** as its complement, as in **It was I who told you**; when it is not the subject or the complement, it assumes the form **me**, or, as possessive, **my**. **He/him, she/her, they/them** and **who/whom** form similar pairs.

(e) PRONOUNS

If a noun-phrase consists of a single word, it is either a *noun* or a *pronoun*. Pronouns form a rather artificial category, comprising words of several distinct kinds. *Personal* pronouns are words like **I**, **he**, **she**, **it** and their plural forms **we** and **they**; the pronoun **you** may be singular or plural. They differ from nouns in serving to determine who or what is being spoken of only by reference to the context: who is speaking, who is being addressed, or who or what was previously mentioned. The words **who**, **whom** and **which** can function either as relative or interrogative pronouns. *Relative* pronouns serve to introduce a relative clause, attaching a subordinate sentence to some noun-phrase in the main sentence. *Interrogative* pronouns serve to form a question: direct as in **Whom did you meet?** or reported (indirect) as in **She asked whom you met**. *Indefinite* pronouns, such as **someone, nothing, everybody, anyone,** do not refer to anything or anybody in particular, but express generality.

(f) Nouns

We have seen how to identify the subject of a sentence. We have seen how to identify a whole phrase as a noun-phrase, namely as one that could be the subject of a sentence. How, then, finally, are we to identify a word within a noun-phrase as a noun? That is essentially easy: the noun is the *principal* word in the noun-phrase. If a noun-phrase does not consist of a single pronoun, or a pronoun with a relative clause attached to it, the principal word it contains will be a *noun*. It may contain more than one noun: a noun-phrase may be part of a longer one. In **the officers' wives,** both **wives** and **officers'** are nouns, and in **the dog which bit the postman,** so are both **dog** and **postman.** The principal noun in the phrase is, however, the word which (supplemented by an article, possessive pronoun like **my** or **their,** or indefinite adjective like **some** or **no**) serves most to tell the hearer what is being talked about: the wives, rather than the officers, the dog, rather than the postman. If there are other nouns in the noun-phrase, they will occur as possessives like **officers'** or within a relative clause like **which bit the postman** or after a preposition like **on, for** or **by** that does not govern the whole noun-phrase. In **He was insulted by the man from the Ministry, the man from the Ministry** is a noun-phrase governed by the preposition **by.** Both **man** and **Ministry** are nouns, but **man** is the principal noun of the phrase, since the preposition **from** does not govern the whole phrase, but only the constituent noun-phrase **the Ministry.** We have not given a watertight definition: but anyone previously unsure which words are nouns should be clear on the matter now.

(g) Adjectives

The remaining 'parts of speech' can be characterised more quickly. *Adjectives* typically serve to add descriptive content, and have two functions. They frequently precede a noun, either with the purpose of specifying the reference or simply with that of making the characterisation more detailed. Thus **lame** and **clever** are adjectives, and occur characteristically in **the lame dog** and **the clever rogue; the lame dog** may be used to indicate which of several dogs is being referred to, whereas, although no more than one rogue was in question, attention needed to be drawn to his acuteness. An adjective can readily be distinguished from a noun by the fact that it cannot by itself form a phrase with **a** before it; a noun must follow. Thus one could not say **a lame** by itself, but only as part of a phrase like **a lame man**. The phrase **the lame**, without a noun to follow it, can be used as a plural term referring to lame people in general, as in **they brought to him the sick, the lame and the blind**. In the singular, it must be followed by a noun, as in **the lame dog**. The second function of adjectives is to follow a verb like **to be** or **to become**, as in **she is clever, he has always been lame** and **he has become lazy** (the adjective here is, of course, **lazy**).

Not all words traditionally classed as adjectives *have* a descriptive content, properly so called. Certain structural words count as adjectives when they play a similar grammatical role. What shows that these words should really be classified as forming a separate category of their own is that they can very often function either like an adjective or like a noun. Good examples are the demonstratives **this** and **that**. They function like adjectives in such phrases as **this hat** and **that table**, and they are then usually called *demonstrative adjectives*; but they can equally well function like nouns, as in **This is very difficult** and **Don't do that!**; they are then called *demonstrative pronouns*. The words **same** (almost invariably preceded by the definite article **the**) and **other** play the same dual role. In **I caught the same train** and **I caught the other train**, they function as adjectives; in **He said the same** and **She turned to the other**, they function as nouns. The possessive forms of the personal pronouns exhibit an interesting peculiarity, in that, in their adjectival use, they assume different forms before a noun and after the verb **to be: He is wearing my tie**, but **That tie is mine**. The second of these forms also functions as a noun, as in **Don't take mine!**

(h) ADVERBS

Adverbs are generally distinguished sharply from adjectives in English. Most of them are easily recognised, because they end in **-ly**, though the adverb **well**, corresponding to the adjective **good**, does not, while **likely** is an adjective; a few adverbs, like **clockwise**, end in **-wise**. (**Well** is of course also used as an adjective, meaning 'in good health'.) Like adjectives, adverbs have two different functions: to qualify verbs, or whole sentences, clauses or phrases, as adjectives qualify nouns; and to modify adjectives or other adverbs. Thus in **He thoroughly scoured the saucepan**, the adverb **thoroughly** can be regarded as qualifying the verb **scoured** (or the whole verb-phrase **scoured the saucepan**); in **Disappointingly, there were no tickets left**, **disappointingly** qualifies the whole of the rest of the sentence; and in **Salt is reputedly unhealthy**, **reputedly** modifies the adjective **unhealthy**. When, in *Kind Hearts and Coronets*, Alec Guinness, as the Rev. the Hon. Ascoyne D'Ascoyne, said **I always say that my west window has all the exuberance of Chaucer, without, happily, any of the concomitant crudity**, he was using **happily** to qualify the phrase **without any of the concomitant crudity**. Some adverbs can perform only the first function: **He plays well**, **We are well out of it** and **She is well dressed** are all proper uses of **well**, but **well proud** and **well strong** are impossible. Conversely, **very** performs only the second function: it can precede an adjective, as in **very quick**, or another adverb, as in **very quickly**, but not a verb.

(i) CONJUNCTIONS

Conjunctions serve to join together clauses (other than relative clauses) or to introduce a subordinate clause. **And** and **or** join two clauses (said to be *co-ordinate*), and are archetypical conjunctions. **Both** may precede the first of two clauses joined by **and**, and **Either** the first of two joined by **or**; **Both ... and** is really then a single (discontinuous) conjunction, and the same holds for **Either ... or**. **But** also conjoins co-ordinate clauses. **If** introduces a *subordinate* clause (the other being the *main* clause); **If ... then** is another discontinuous conjunction. **Although** and **because** also introduce subordinate clauses. All these conjunctions can, however, join words or phrases shorter than whole clauses, as in **man and beast** or **both man and beast**, **naughty but nice**, **borrowed or stole** or **either borrowed or stole**, **if and when**, **charming because unspoiled**, **in the country although near to town**. All that is required is that the two words or phrases should be of the same grammatical category.

Conjunctions of comparison, like **than** and **as**, do not need to stand directly between the words or phrases they connect: in **Hercules was stronger than Samson**, **than** connects (compares) **Hercules** with **Samson**; in **Susan is not so young as Joan**, **as** connects (compares) **Susan** with **Joan**.

That introduces a clause reporting someone's statement, belief or the like: the clause is said to be in *indirect speech*. **Whether** similarly introduces a reported Yes/No question. When used in this way, **that** and **whether** can govern only whole clauses, not lesser phrases.

(j) PREPOSITIONS

A transitive verb expresses a relationship between two people or things, or the occurrence of an event involving two people or things; but some relationships hold between more than two people or things, and some events involve more than two people or things. Thus two people and a thing are involved in the actions reported by **She gave a scarf to her husband** and by **He borrowed the book from his sister**. The words **to** and **from** are *prepositions*. By a change in word order, saying **She gave her husband a scarf**, we can dispense with the **to** in the first sentence; here **a scarf** is said to be the *direct object* of the verb, and **her husband** the *indirect object*. But the preposition **from** cannot be dispensed with. Prepositions, which are mostly rather short words, thus serve to indicate the role of a person or thing in a relationship or action. When a sentence is converted from active to passive form, what was previously the object becomes the subject, and what was previously the subject comes to be governed by the preposition **by**: **The farmer led the horse** becomes **The horse was led by the farmer**.

Giving and borrowing obviously involve two people and a thing; but it is difficult to say just how many things *are* involved in actions and events. An event must take place somewhere and at some time; an action is usually performed by means of some implement or with some purpose. All these are indicated by phrases beginning with a preposition: in the sentence **He buttered the toast** *with* **a knife** *in* **the kitchen** *on* **Saturday** *for* **the party** the prepositions have been italicised.

(k) INTERJECTIONS

Interjections are short words standing at the beginning of a sentence, not contributing to the content but setting a mood; examples are **Oh**, as in **Oh, must we?**, **Well**, as in **Well, it depends what you want it for**, and **Now**, as in **Now Barabbas was a robber**.

2. Some Grammatical Principles

(a) ACCUSATIVE AND NOMINATIVE

I begin with notes on two pairs of grammatical terms, whose use could not be avoided here, in case they confuse anyone. Many languages employ inflection; this consists in changing the form of a word, particularly its termination, to modify its meaning or indicate its grammatical role; it is used in English in forming plurals. Most Indo-European languages inflect pronouns, and many inflect nouns and their accompanying adjectives and participles, according to their 'case', that is, their function in the sentence. The two most important cases are the *nominative* and the *accusative*.

The *nominative* is used for the subject of a verb, and also for the complement of a verb like **is, was** or **becomes** (the complement of such a verb being the pronoun or noun-phrase following it).

The *accusative* is used for the object of a verb (see 2(f)), and also, in English, for a noun or pronoun governed by a preposition, such as **by, with, to, from** and similar words.

Inflection for case has almost disappeared from English: there are only eight words in the language that have different forms for the nominative and accusative cases, all of them pronouns. These are **I/me, he/him, she/her, we/us, they/them, who/whom, whoever/whomever** and **whosoever/whomsoever** (formerly also **thou/thee** and **ye/you**). Although case plays so slight a role in determining the form of the word used, a mistake about the form of any of these eight words gives a very bad appearance to a piece of writing. Common mistakes of this kind are as follows.

He who, she who. The now somewhat archaic **he who** has the sense of 'anyone who', *not* of 'someone who' as used when the reference is to a single person. Thus Bunyan wrote:

Who would true valour see,
Let him come hither;

this, like its prose equivalent **Let him who would see true valour come hither**, means 'Let anyone come hither who would see true valour'. We could not say **Mr Standfast was he who wanted to see true valour**; it ought to be **Mr Standfast was one who wanted to see true valour**.

The phrase **he who** (or **she who**) has lately become fashionable again; but it is frequently misused. A characteristic example is **The referendum is only the penultimate refuge of she who has lost the party's support** (letter in the *Guardian*, 27 November 1991). **She who** is here wrongly used as referring to a particular person (Mrs. Thatcher); **someone, one** or **the one** is needed in place of **she**.

Furthermore, as this example also illustrates, grammar is almost invariably flouted. The case of the relative pronoun **who** is determined by its function in the relative clause that it governs; if it is the subject of that clause, the form **who** (instead of **whom**) is therefore correct. But the case of the pronoun **he** or **she** should be determined by its function in the main clause: if it is the object of that clause, or is governed by a preposition, it should take the form **him** or **her**, as in the above quotation from Bunyan, or in the tag **All things come to him who waits**. Thus **Retribution will overtake he who commits a murder** and **It is an opportunity for he who wishes to be famous** embody grammatical howlers; **he** should be replaced by **him** in both cases. **She denounced he who had committed the murder** embodies both mistakes, since here the murderer is a particular person, even though it may not be known who he is. **She denounced whoever had committed the murder** captures the required sense.

The opposite mistake also sometimes occurs, as in **it was him who gave Harris his orders** (letter in the *Observer*, 7 June 1992). In colloquial speech a pronoun is often put into the accusative after the verb **to be**, as in **It's me**, to function like the emphatic pronoun in French (**C'est moi**); but this should not be done in writing. It should of course have been **it was he who gave Harris his orders**. (See 2(e) for further remarks about relative clauses and pronouns.)

We. A curious impression is abroad concerning **we**, namely that it is indeclinable when it precedes a noun or noun-phrase (as in **we Britons**); a typical example is **eternal verities lost to we bloated sophisticates** (D. Stafford, *Guardian*, 16 November 1991). There is no truth to this: if the pronoun should be **us** if it stood alone, it should be **us** when followed by a noun-phrase. Some people have the opposite illusion, exemplified by **what us women think about** (from a letter in the *Catholic Herald*, 5 June 1992): if the pronoun should be **we** if it stood alone, it should be **we** when followed by a noun-phrase. We should therefore have **lost to us bloated sophisticates** and **what we women think about.**

Who and whom. A common mistake is to use **whom** instead of **who** before **I believe, he said** and the like.

Examples are **a young prince whom she believes could have inspired** ... (M. Bailey, *Observer,* October 1991) and **a woman whom I was quite sure was Mrs Kettering's maid** (Agatha Christie, 1928). In such cases, the relative pronoun is the subject of the relative clause, and should therefore have the form **who**; the phrase **she believes, I was quite sure** or the like is best considered as parenthetical, as would appear clearly if it were enclosed in commas – **a young prince who, she believes, could have inspired** ... and **a woman who, I was quite sure, was Mrs Kettering's maid.**

The forms quoted from Martin Bailey and Agatha Christie are as ungrammatical as **She believes him could have inspired** ... and **I was quite sure her was Mrs Kettering's maid,** and for exactly the same reason. The confusion arises because verbs like **to believe** can be transitive (see 2(f)); but they then need to be followed by an infinitive, as in **I believed her to be the maid** and **whom I believed to be the maid.** In the latter case, **I** really is the subject of the relative clause, instead of merely appearing to be so, as in Agatha Christie's phrase.

Of the two ungrammatical examples cited, that by Agatha Christie is the worse, because **to be sure** can never act as a transitive verb; one cannot say **I was quite sure her to be the maid.** This well illustrates how one mistake, habitually made, can lead to a yet worse mistake. (See 2(e) for further remarks about relative clauses and pronouns.)

Whoever and whomever. **Whoever** governs a relative clause. It has two meanings: sometimes it means 'anyone who', and sometimes 'the one who', where the speaker is unable or unwilling to specify the person in other terms. Its case is like that of **who**: that is to say, it is in the nominative if it is the subject of the relative clause, in the accusative if it is the object of that clause. When **whoever** is used, the pronoun belonging to the main clause is understood (i.e. tacit).

It is therefore wrong to write **whomever** just because the tacit pronoun preceding **whoever** should be in the accusative, as is nowadays commonly done. **She denounced whomever had committed the crime** and **I**

dedicate this to whomever invented the wheel thus embody grammatical howlers.

In both cases, the form needed is **whoever**, because it is the subject of **had committed the crime** and **invented the wheel** respectively. This is the opposite mistake to that common with **he who**. (See 2(e) for further remarks.)

You and I. It is increasingly common to hear and read phrases like **to you and I**. This is a false genteelism: it arises from instructions that it is politer to say **you and I** than **I and you**, which indeed it is. The principle is then quite wrongly generalised as requiring the first-person singular pronoun to be in the nominative case whenever preceded by **and**.

The fact that **I** is conjoined to **you**, or to any other noun or pronoun, has no bearing on its case, however. Where the word on its own would be **me**, the phrase should be **you and me** (or **him and me**, etc.); only where, with only the one pronoun, it would be right to use **I** is it right to say **you and I**, **he and I** or **Smith and I**.

The genitive case. In addition to the nominative and accusative cases, there is also a genitive or possessive case. Ordinary nouns have a distinct genitive or possessive form; this is formed by adding **'s** to a plural noun, like **men** or **women**, that does not end with **s**, or to any singular noun, and a simple apostrophe to a plural noun ending in **s**: thus **a man's hat, a fox's tail, women's hats** and **foxes' tails**.

Possessive personal pronouns have two forms: those that function like adjectives, and those that function much as nouns. The adjectival ones are **my, your, his, her, its, our, their** and, when used, **thy**. The substantival ones are **mine, yours, his, hers, its, ours, theirs** and, when used, **thine**. The possessive form of the relative pronouns **who** and **which** is **whose**. See also under *Apostrophes* in Section 4.

(b) ADJECTIVES AND ADVERBS

Most readers will be familiar with the distinction between these two grammatical categories or 'parts of speech'; but anyone in the least unsure of it needs to get a firm grasp on it, since otherwise grammatical mistakes will be unavoidable.

An adjective is used after a verb like **to be** or **to become** as the complement of a noun, pronoun or noun-phrase, as the adjective **rapid** is used in **The advance was very rapid.** It is also used as part of a noun-phrase to qualify the noun, as the adjective **hypothetical** is used within the noun-phrase **the hypothetical inventor of the zip fastener.**

An adverb is used to qualify a verb, as **rapidly** is used in **They advanced rapidly,** an entire clause, as **allegedly** is used in **They allegedly used it to launder drug profits,** or an adjective or other adverb, as **remarkably** is used in **The business is remarkably lucrative** and **She walked remarkably quickly.**

English draws a sharp distinction between adjectives and adverbs; among the few words to have the same form when used in either way are **fast, long, hard, late** and **early,** which can be adjectives as in **a fast car, a long time, a hard row** and **his late arrival,** or adverbs as in **He drives too fast, It did not last long, She works very hard** and **He arrived late.**

Recently the distinction between adjectives and adverbs appears to have become blurred in the minds of many, as when **such** is used in place of **so,** or **other** in place of **otherwise.** The tendency to ignore the distinction between adjectives and adverbs doubtless results from the influence on British speakers and writers of American speech, in turn strongly influenced by German, which hardly recognises a difference between adjectives and adverbs, whereas the tradition of the English language is to make a firm distinction between them. Phrases like **to act natural** and **he doesn't see good** are pure Germanisms, and, though in common use by Americans, are recognised as slang; other examples are more subtle and go unrecognised by most American writers and increasingly by British ones. Particular cases of the tendency are as follows.

Other. **Other** is an adjective, and cannot ever properly be used as an adverb; it should always have a noun to qualify. You can say **He could see no solution other than to go by train,** because in this sentence **other** qualifies **solution**; and you can likewise say **He could do nothing other than persist with his story,** because here **other** qualifies **nothing,** which is grammatically a noun. But you cannot say **He is unable to act other than ungraciously,** because in that sentence **other** has no noun to qualify. What it is intended to qualify is the *verb* **act,** and what qualifies a verb is an adverb, not an adjective.

Mathematics cannot treat of the infinite other than via the principles ... (M. Tiles, 1991), **Few newspaper proprietors ... relish causing discomfort to miscreant power-brokers other than when ...** (T. Bower, *Guardian,* 9 December 1991) and **It is difficult to avoid devel-**

oping **properties of dimension other than in a way that applies to 'fractal' and 'non-fractal' sets alike** (K. Falconer, 1990) all embody the same widespread mistake. The adverb corresponding to **other** is **otherwise**, which the grammatically insensitive continue to use in contexts like **otherwise there will be** … and **otherwise known as** … , but from which they drop the adverbial ending **-wise** before **than**. Grammar would therefore be satisfied by making the sentences run **He is unable to act otherwise than ungraciously, Mathematics cannot treat of the infinite otherwise than via the principles** … , **Few newspaper proprietors** … **relish causing discomfort to miscreant power-brokers otherwise than when** … and **It is difficult to avoid developing properties of dimension otherwise than in a way** … .

The replacement of **other** by **otherwise** is often not the best solution, however; the last three examples illustrate the fact that **otherwise than** is seldom needed save when what follows **than** is a single adverb. The two words may frequently be better replaced by the single word **except** or **save**. Thus in the three foregoing sentences, **save via the principles**, **except when** and **save in a way** would be a distinct improvement on **otherwise than via the principles**, **otherwise than when** and **otherwise than in a way**.

Clumsiness can also often be avoided by using **other** grammatically, as an adjective; for instance, in the last of the four examples, by writing **in a way other than one that applies**. A simple negative will also often suffice: **in any way that does not apply** would do equally well.

Such, so. **Such** is an adjective, **so** an adverb. **In such a manner, to such an extent** and **to such a degree** can all be expressed simply by **so**. They cannot be expressed simply by **such**, however, which, being an adjective, must have a noun to qualify. It is therefore wrong to write **She insulted most of her supporters such that they eventually drove her from office**; what is needed is **She so insulted her supporters that they eventually drove her from office**. This mistake has also become rife in very recent years. **She directed such insults at her supporters that they eventually drove her from office** is, of course, quite correct.

Prior and subsequent. **Prior** and **subsequent** are adjectives. One may therefore legitimately say **The axioms are prior to the domain** or **The domain is subsequent to the axioms**. The common habit of using **prior to** as a compound preposition introducing an adverbial phrase, as in **Prior**

to setting out, he checked the ammunition**, is a gross solecism: what is
wanted in place of **prior to** is the familiar preposition **before**.

Similarly, one should not write **The axioms are given prior to the
domain** or **The domain is given only subsequent to the axioms** (M.
Tiles). In the latter case, either **subsequent** should be replaced by **subsequently**, or **subsequent to** by **after**. There is no adverbial form of **prior**;
again, **before** will do very well in place of **prior to**.

The same. **The same,** whether used adjectivally or as a noun-phrase,
requires completion by **as,** not by **that. He used the same words as I had**
and **He used the very words that I had** are both correct (as is **He used
the very same words as I had**); **He used the same words that I had** is
wrong. **The same** cannot be used as an adverbial phrase: you cannot say
they function the same, but only **they function in the same way. He did
the same** is, of course, entirely proper, since **to do** is a transitive verb, and
here **the same** is not adverbial, but a noun-phrase forming the object of
did.

First, secondly. **First** can be either an adjective, as in **the first man
on the moon,** or an adverb, as in **He first filled the kettle and then put
it on the stove.** The form **firstly** is therefore as redundant as **fastly** would
be, and should never be used. **Second, third** and so on can only be
adjectives. Hence an enumeration of points should proceed: **First, ...
Secondly, ... Thirdly, ...** The (fairly rare) exception occurs when there
is a definite noun for the ordinal numerals to qualify, in which case we
need **first, ... , second, ... , third:** an example is **He made three
objections: first, that ... ; second, that ... ; and, third, that ....**

In depth. The phrase **in depth** prompts grammatical errors. The phrase
is an adverbial one, designed for use in such an expression as **to study
animal behaviour in depth,** which is accordingly grammatically correct.
It ought therefore not to be used as an adjectival phrase, as in **a more in
depth analysis.** If it is to be so used, it ought at least to be hyphenated;
but, since the language contains the adjective **deep,** there is no need to use
it in this way at all: **a deeper analysis** is plainer and better English. **In
depth** qualifies as a cliché, and is for that reason better avoided altogether.
Thus **to make a deep study of animal behaviour** would be a fresher
phrasing than **to study animal behaviour in depth**.

Way. **Way** is a noun, and should not be used as an adverb, as in **way above**; the correct adverb here is **far**. **A long way above** is unobjectionable.

Comparison of adjectives. Save for **worse**, comparative adjectives are usually formed by adding **-er** to the simple form, or putting **more** in front of it, and are followed by **than** to indicate the term to which the comparison is being made. These should properly be called 'superior comparatives'; inferior comparatives are formed by putting **less** in front of the simple form, and are also followed by **than**.

Than should not be replaced by **compared to** or **in comparison with**, as in **how much worse British sit-coms are compared to American ones** (Toby Young, *Guardian*, 7 April 1992); or, if it is, the adjective should be in the simple, not the comparative form, since the prepositional phrase says that a comparison is being made. Thus, we should have either **how much worse British sit-coms are than American ones** or **how bad British sit-coms are compared to American ones**.

Similarly, it is wrong to prefix **rather** to **than** in such contexts. **Rather**, which is etymologically a comparative, behaves as itself a comparative adverb, as in **I would rather walk than go by bus**, and **rather than** is virtually synonymous with **instead of**. The intrusion of **rather** in an ordinary comparison therefore alters the sense; it is inadvisable to use **rather**, however correctly, in a sentence in which there is another comparative, for fear of misunderstanding.

A good example is **By this time I was doing a little teaching, … so felt more relaxed when talking to Blunt about the world in general rather than simply asking him scholarly questions** (T. Hilton, *Guardian*, 11 April 1992). If **rather** has here been incorrectly inserted, the writer means that he felt more relaxed when talking about the world in general than when asking scholarly questions. But if **rather** is being used correctly, he means that at that time he felt more relaxed when talking to Blunt than he had formerly done. The ambiguity cannot be resolved: it could have been avoided by deleting **rather** in the first case, or replacing **rather than** by **instead of** in the second.

The adverbs **how** and **so** cannot precede a comparative adjective directly, as in **What is so apparent about this Los Angeles riot is not how different, or how worse, it is from Watts but how depressingly similar** (A. Hamilton, *Observer*, 3 May 1992): they require to be followed by **much** (**how much worse, so much better**). The quoted sentence needs further revision, since **worse** cannot govern **from**: ... **not how different it is from Watts, nor how much worse, but how depressingly similar** would suffice.

Note that **than** is a conjunction, not a preposition: hence the correct form is **She is cleverer than I**, not **She is cleverer than me** (see 2(e)).

(c) TWO TYPES OF ADVERBS

There are two ways in which adverbs may be used, as may be seen from the different meanings of **Disgracefully, he failed every paper** and **He failed every paper disgracefully**. The first means that it was disgraceful that he failed every paper (even if he failed each one by only a narrow margin); the second means that, for each paper, he failed it by a disgracefully wide margin. **He disgracefully failed every paper**, though grammatical, is ambiguous between the two, and should therefore be avoided; **He failed disgracefully every paper** is not English, having a word-order that sounds unnatural to every native speaker. Similarly with **Disgracefully, there was no paper that he passed**; one could say **There was, disgracefully, no paper that he passed**, but the commas would be essential and the sentence clumsy.

Adverbs, or uses of them, are of two distinct types. Most qualify the verb or verbal phrase in the way an adjective qualifies a noun, often by stating the manner in which the relevant event took place, as in **She hurriedly picked up the plate**; but others qualify the *whole clause*, indicating either its status as a fact or otherwise (as do **probably, presumably** and **allegedly**) or (like **surprisingly**) a judgement upon that fact. A sentence containing an adverb playing the second role can always be transformed into one of the form **It is ... that** or **It is ... of ... to**. For instance, **Disgracefully, he failed every paper** implies **It was disgraceful that he failed every paper**, while **She wittily replied ...** means **It was witty of her to reply ... Presumably** is only an apparent exception to this principle, due to our not using the form **It is presumable that**, but only **It is to be presumed that**.

Some adverbs (like **carelessly, wittily** and **disgracefully**) can fulfil either role, according to their placing in the sentence. In general, an adverb playing the first role comes late in the sentence, one playing the second early on. Hence, if you want **carelessly** to indicate the manner in which something was done, i.e. to play the first role, you must place it at the end: **She picked up the plate carelessly** means that she picked up the plate in a careless fashion. But if you put **carelessly** before the verb, you will confer on it its second role: **She carelessly picked up the plate** means that it was careless of her to pick up the plate at all.

An adverb that can play only one of these roles can occupy different positions without ambiguity. Thus **hurriedly** can play only the first of the two roles; it makes no sense to say that it was hurried of someone to do something. Hence a sentence like **She hurriedly picked up the plate**, in which **hurriedly** is placed before the verb, has the same sense as **She picked up the plate hurriedly,** and is even slightly more natural. Likewise, **presumably** can play only the second role; so the three sentences **Presumably, he will arrive tomorrow, He will presumably arrive tomorrow** and **He will arrive tomorrow, presumably** mean the same. It is the placing of adverbs that can play both roles that can alter the sense, and hence needs care.

Of the pair **regretfully** and **regrettably**, the former, meaning **with regret,** can play only the first role, and the latter only the second. **Regrettably, none of the Fellows knows Hungarian** implies that it is regrettable – to be regretted – that none of the Fellows knows Hungarian; **Regretfully, none of the Fellows knows Hungarian** makes no sense, because it is not *regretful* that none of the Fellows knows Hungarian, and does not make sense to say that it is. A state of affairs may be disgraceful, but only a person can be regretful; hence **regretfully** can be used only in such contexts as **I have regretfully to tell you that the ink is soaking into the carpet.** If it meant anything, **The ink is regretfully soaking into the carpet** would mean that the ink felt regrets about soaking into the carpet.

Of late **regretfully** has come often to be used in the sense of **regrettably.** This has happened under the influence of **hopefully,** which used to be understood as meaning 'in a hopeful spirit', as in **To travel hopefully is better than to arrive,** and thus used in the first of the two adverbial roles; but now it has come to replace **I hope** or **it is to be hoped,** as in **The shop will hopefully be open.** In this usage, ineffectually combated by purists, the proverb would have the sense 'It is to be hoped that it is better to travel than to arrive'. The innovation is to be regretted, because the analogy with this new use prompts people wantonly to misuse other words like **regretfully,** causing confusion in the process and damaging the language. The purists failed, however, to notice or resist an earlier change in the use of **thankfully. The refugees thankfully boarded the vessel** means that the refugees were thankful that they were boarding it; **Thankfully, the refugees boarded the vessel** may well be intended to mean that the *speaker* is thankful that they did. This second use of **thankfully** already broke the purity of the principle stated above, in that it is not thankful that the refugees boarded the vessel: only a person can be thankful, not a state of affairs. Likewise, only a person can be hopeful; it is not hopeful that the shop will be open. The new use of **hopefully** cannot now be dislodged; but it is still better to avoid it when possible, and, when not, to place **hopefully**, so understood, at the beginning of the sentence.

(d) PARTICIPLES AND GERUNDS

The termination **-ing**, added to the root of a verb, serves to form two essentially different verbal expressions: a participle and a gerund. These are *grammatically* different: a participle is essentially an adjective, a gerund a noun. They can therefore be distinguished by their role in the sentence that contains them, that is, by the behaviour of the other words in the sentence; since they have exactly the same form, they can *only* be so distinguished. To ignore the grammatical difference between them is therefore to cause, or to invite, confusion. To decide which is which, one needs to think exactly what one means, but this is no bad thing; everyone should cultivate the habit, when writing, of always thinking whether what he has written says just what he intended to say.

In **We passed a man struggling up the hill on his bicycle**, **struggling** is functioning as an adjective qualifying **a man**; similarly with **We passed Jones struggling up the hill on his bicycle** and **We passed him struggling up the hill on his bicycle**. In these sentences, therefore, **struggling** is a *participle*.

A good test for its being one is to check that the whole sentence implies the shorter sentence that results from deleting the participial phrase. In the cases given, it does: for instance, **We passed Jones struggling up the hill on his bicycle** implies **We passed Jones**. Because, in these sentences, **struggling** is a participle, functioning as a qualifying adjective, the object of the verb in each case is the noun, noun-phrase or pronoun. The only one of these three kinds of expression that takes a different form in the nominative and accusative cases (when it is the subject and when it is the object) is a pronoun: in the third sentence above, **him** is therefore correctly in the accusative case.

In a sentence like **The undergraduates resent paying a higher rent** or **The undergraduates object to paying a higher rent,** there is no noun or noun-phrase for **paying** to qualify. It is therefore functioning as itself a noun, and is a gerund, not a participle. The whole phrase **paying a higher rent** is thus the object of the verb **resent** in the first sentence, and is what the preposition governs in the second; it is itself a noun-phrase.

A misunderstanding of this fact will not show up in sentences like these; but it will show up if the sentence mentions an agent, as in **The undergraduates object to the College's imposing a higher rent.** It is because **imposing** is a gerund, and thus a sort of noun, that the possessive form is needed for the noun indicating the agent: the form **The undergraduates object to the College imposing a higher rent** is as incorrect as **He stole him pen,** and for the same reason. The undergraduates do not object to the College, as an institution, but to its action in imposing a higher rent; and therefore the phrase should be in its possessive form, **the College's.** By contrast, we passed *Jones*, not his struggling.

The same holds good for **He concealed my being in debt from my parents; He concealed me being in debt from my parents** could only mean that, while I was in debt, he hid me so that my parents could not find me, whereas what was meant was that he concealed, not me, but the fact that I was in debt. Similarly, again, with **It was due to my visiting Venice that I met the girl I adore;** the sentence **It was due to me visiting Venice that I met the girl I adore** would imply that the merit was mine. The same test can be applied as before: the sentence **It was due to me visiting Venice that I met the girl I adore,** wrongly used, is not intended to imply **It was due to me that I met the girl I adore;** and so **visiting** is not a participle, but a gerund, and the **me** ought to be **my.** A good example of the common confusion between participle and gerund occurs in **Despite Morocco accepting a detailed peace plan, it has continuously violated the terms of the agreement** (letter by Glenys Kinnock in the *Guardian*, 30 January 1992); **Despite accepting a detailed peace plan, Morocco has continuously violated** ... would have been grammatical.

A verbal noun-phrase with a gerund is intrinsically ambiguous between 'the fact that ... ' and 'the manner in which ... '. The ambiguity seldom arises in practice, however: almost always the former is unmistakably meant. An exception occurs in sentences like **His acting is polished,** where the gerund stands on its own, and has almost attained the status of an independent noun. The suggestion has been made that a phrase with a gerund always has the sense of 'the manner in which ... ', so that **I do not like his singing** can only mean 'I do not like the way he sings', and we have to say **I do not like him singing** if we mean 'I do not like him to sing at all'. This is quite wrong; the principle would rule out almost all uses of the gerund. On the few occasions when such an ambiguity occurs, it is best avoided by the use of an unambiguous phrase.

I saw him going into the Randolph Hotel is something of a special case. Here **going** is a participle, and so **him** is correct. The form with the gerund, **I saw his going into the Randolph Hotel,** on the other hand, is not possible. This is one of the rare instances in which an infinitive is used without **to: I saw him go into the Randolph Hotel.** Other examples are with verbs like **make** and **let: I made him tell the truth,** and **She let me hold her hand.**

There is, of course, a nuance. **I saw him go into the Randolph Hotel** says that I have visual evidence for his going into the Randolph Hotel; it is therefore appropriate when what is primarily in question is whether he went into the Randolph Hotel. **I saw him going into the Randolph Hotel,** on the other hand, says merely that I saw him, and that he was going into the Randolph Hotel at the time; it would be appropriate when what was in question was whether he was around at all.

Another test that can be applied in cases of uncertainty is to turn the sentence round so that the noun or pronoun governing the verb in **-ing** becomes the subject. **I saw him wearing a smoking jacket** becomes **He was seen wearing a smoking jacket,** and so the **him** in the original sentence was quite correct. But **We were surprised by him wearing a smoking jacket** would become **He surprised us wearing a smoking jacket,** which is obviously wrong: it should be either **He surprised us by wearing a smoking jacket** or **His wearing a smoking jacket surprised us;** hence **him** in the original sentence should be **his.**

Almost all of this entry was written before I became aware that this point, like the split infinitive, has become a focus of active resistance to objectors: the authority of Jespersen is invoked to license locutions like **Despite Morocco accepting.** Those belonging to this maquis deliberately use **him** instead of **his,** etc., on all possible occasions, just as defenders of the split infinitive leave no infinitive unsplit if they can avoid it. Thus an article by Peter Taylor in the *Independent Magazine* for 18 July 1992 is marred by **the chances of them staying sober** and **points clearly to it being** ... : the article is otherwise so well written that these are very probably intentional.

Such phrases grate on my ear: on others, doubtless, the forms with **their** and **its** would sound a trifle stilted. The question both factions must ask themselves is whether we do more service to the language by making the use of the possessive obsolete in these contexts, or by following the rule here stated. In a recent book I wrote a sentence I will here abridge as **He repudiated the possibility of a semantic theory explaining how sentences are determined as true or as false**; it does not matter for present purposes what this remark is about. I meant that he repudiated the possibility of a semantic theory altogether, such a theory being one that would explain .... But when I read the sentence through in proof, I realised, what would not have occurred to me a few years ago, that many readers would take me to mean that he repudiated the possibility that a semantic theory could explain .... If I had meant that, I should have written **of a semantic theory's explaining**; but the loss of a sense of the distinction between participle and gerund made it likely that I should be misunderstood. (Insertion of a comma after **theory** would have warded off this ambiguity, at the cost of introducing another: taking the participle **explaining** to attach to the pronoun **He**.) In many contexts, the use of the accusative in place of the possessive will create no ambiguity; but the obliteration of a grammatical distinction will almost always render ambiguous some sentences that were not ambiguous before. Good reason is therefore needed if we are to set about obliterating it; in the present case, no such reason is apparent.

Dangling participles. In June 1991 a reviewer in a Sunday paper vilified a novelist for using 'dangling participles', and illustrated the vice by quoting two sentences from her novel; in neither was the participle dangling. A dangling participle is one occurring in a sentence that contains no noun or pronoun that it is meant to qualify. This is not a stylistic but a *grammatical* mistake; a participle, being a verbal adjective, can no more lack a noun to qualify than can an ordinary adjective. An example is **Taking the broad view, Napoleon did more good than harm**: what it *says* is that Napoleon, when taking the broad view, did more good than harm, whereas it is the writer who intends to be understood as taking a broad view. **Napoleon** is here the only available noun for **taking** to be attached to, and so, grammatically construed, the sentence can only be understood as attributing the broad view to the Emperor.

Those who know Latin may be encouraged by the fact that, if the hymn 'Adoro te devote' is rightly attributed to St. Thomas Aquinas, he was guilty of a dangling participle: **Quia te contemplans totum deficit**, a line difficult to translate while preserving the grammatical solecism.

A common recent form of dangling participle is **having said that,** as in **Having said that, the original question remains unanswered.** Strictly interpreted, this can only mean that the *question* just made the remark referred to; of course, it was the writer (or speaker) who did so. Instead of a participial phrase, what is needed is **Despite that,** or some similar expression. **Having said that, I have to admit that ...** is, of course, quite correct, since **having said that** attaches to the pronoun **I.**

A participle dangles whenever that which it is meant to qualify is not in fact mentioned in the sentence in which it occurs, whether or not that is the speaker. An example is **Stripped of her more lurid language, Baroness Thatcher has a point** (P. Kellner, *Independent*, 3 July 1992). The writer means that, when Lady Thatcher's observations have been stripped of their lurid wording, they contain a point; what he has said is that when *she* is stripped of her lurid language, she has a point.

(e) PREPOSITIONS AND CONJUNCTIONS

A preposition (**from, by, with,** etc.) may govern a pronoun or a noun-phrase; it serves to indicate a relation between what the pronoun or noun-phrase refers to and another thing mentioned, or its role in the situation described. The resulting phrase, consisting of the preposition together with the pronoun or noun-phrase it governs, plays the role either of an adjective or an adverb. Thus in **He kissed her in the garden,** the phrase **in the garden** is an adverbial phrase (one playing the role of an adverb): it qualifies the verb-phrase **kissed her.** In **the statue in the garden,** on the other hand, it is an adjectival phrase (one playing the role of an adjective): it specifies which statue is meant.

In this way one phrase formed by means of a preposition, say **in the garden,** may be part of another such phrase, say **to the statue in the garden.** The pronoun after a preposition may be of any kind: a personal pronoun (e.g. **me** or **them**), a relative or interrogative pronoun (e.g. **whom**) or a demonstrative pronoun (e.g. **this**). If it inflects, it must be in the accusative case, as in these examples. A noun-phrase consists of a noun, with or without an article (**a** or **the**) or quantitative adjective (**some, all, no**), and with or without a qualifying adjective, participle, relative clause or adjectival phrase; for instance **some thin women, a sleeping dog, the man who came to dinner, the statue in the garden.**

There are few general principles governing the use of prepositions after verbs, adjectives or nouns: why should we **forbear to cheer** but **refrain**

from cheering? It is notorious that, in learning a foreign language, the choice of preposition is one of the hardest things to master. Using the wrong one therefore makes the user appear a foreigner; but many native speakers now use English as if they were foreigners. Every left-hand page of a form recently circulated to teaching members of Oxford University was headed **Notes of Guidance**; Quest Hair Research advertises **The Natural Cure to Baldness**: surely a native English speaker would have written **Notes** *for* **Guidance** and **The Natural Cure** *for* **Baldness**. Those who use the wrong preposition risk being complimented on how well they speak English.

A relative clause plays the role of an adjective qualifying a noun. It always contains a relative pronoun (**who, whom** or **which, whose** followed by a noun, or **that** used in the sense of **who, whom** or **which**), or with such a pronoun understood; in **the man we saw, whom** or **that** is understood before **we**, and hence **we saw** forms a relative clause, the whole expression **the man we saw** constituting a noun-phrase. The pronoun **what** may be interrogative, as in **What do you want?** or **He did not know what she wanted**; when governing a relative clause, as in **That is not what I was looking for,** it is equivalent to 'that which'. Relative clauses often, but by no means always, start with the relative pronoun.

A relative clause can be transformed into a grammatical sentence by replacing the relative pronoun by a personal pronoun (**who** by **he** or **she, whom** by **him** or **her, which** by **it** and **whose** by **his, her** or **its**) and making appropriate changes to the word order when the relative pronoun was not in the nominative. Thus the relative clause **who came to dinner** becomes the sentence **He came to dinner**, the clause **whom we saw** becomes **We saw her**, etc.; we may call this the 'corresponding' sentence. Whether an expression is part of the relative clause can be decided by asking whether it would belong to the corresponding sentence. In **The explorer, to rescue whom she had come so far, received her coldly,** the sentence corresponding to the relative clause is **She had come so far to rescue him**; the relative clause therefore consists of everything between the commas. An increasingly common mistake is to use **which** instead of **who** or **whom** in reference to people (e.g. **his English friends, not the least of which was Russell**).

The pronouns **who** and **which**, with their inflected forms **whom** and **whose**, can also be used as interrogative pronouns, as in **Whose bat did you borrow?** and **Which did you choose?**; in addition, **which** can be used as an interrogative adjective, as in **Which cake did you choose?**, while **what** can properly be used as an interrogative pronoun or adjective, as in **What did you say?** and **What time is it?**, but *not* as a relative adjective. All these can be used to form indirect question-clauses, like **He asked whose bat you borrowed** and **She did not know what time it was**.

All other clauses are introduced by conjunctions (**and, or, because, although, that**); that is to say, all clauses other than relative clauses and indirect question-clauses governed by **who(m), whose, which** or **what**. It is the typical role of a conjunction to introduce a clause, and all conjunctions are capable of doing so. A clause must contain a finite form of a verb, a finite form being one that is not a participle, gerund or infinitive.

Clauses introduced by conjunctions are often grammatically complete sentences (apart from the conjunction); thus in **Although the professed aim of the Bill is to help refugees, its real purpose is to deter them** the (concessive) clause includes everything up to the comma, and **The professed aim of the Bill is to help refugees**, when detached from the context, forms a complete sentence. In certain cases some changes are needed to arrive at the corresponding sentence. Thus in a conditional clause (one governed by **if**), English idiomatically converts the future into the present tense, for example in **If you meet Sam tomorrow** (Italian uses the future tense in such a clause). **You meet Sam tomorrow** is not, properly speaking, the corresponding sentence, which is obviously **You will meet Sam tomorrow**. Again, **any** may be used in a conditional clause like **If you have read any of his books**, where **some** would be used in a declarative sentence standing on its own; the corresponding sentence is **You have read some of his books** (not **You have read any of his books**).

Some clauses put the verb into the subjunctive, which would not do were the clause removed from its context; **I wish that I were young again** is grammatical, but not **I were young again**; we need **I am young again**. A clause beginning **that** may need some adjustment of the tenses, e.g. from the conditional mood to the future tense: the sentence corresponding to the clause introduced by **that** in **She said that she would meet me** is **She will meet me**.

The word **that** can be a demonstrative adjective (as in **That problem is too hard**), a demonstrative pronoun (as in **That is the question**), a relative pronoun going proxy for **who(m), which, when** or **where** (as in **The argument that he gave** and **the year that King Uzziah died**) or a conjunction. When used as a conjunction, it is exceptional in that it can govern only a whole clause.

A clause introduced by **that** is a kind of noun-phrase, serving, for example, as the object of a verb like **said** or **believes**. It can also be the subject of a sentence, as in **That the object of the Bill is to deter refugees is undeniable**, idiomatically expressible by **It is undeniable that the object of the Bill is to deter refugees**. But, although such a clause functions as a noun-phrase, it will not readily tolerate having a preposition prefixed to it. We say **I was convinced of his innocence**, but **I was convinced that he was innocent**, not **I was convinced of that he was innocent**.

Likewise, we may say **That she was there implies that she never went to Paris**, but not **From that she was there it can be inferred that she never went to Paris**: it must be either **From the fact that she was there** or **From her being there**. It is idiomatic to omit **that** after common verbs like **say**, **think** and even **believe** and **suppose**. It should not be omitted when to do so would cause confusion, for instance when the first word of the clause is **that** used as a demonstrative adjective or pronoun: if someone says, 'That building is unnecessary', his remark cannot be reported in writing without ambiguity by **He said that building was unnecessary**. This would be possible in speech, because the conjunction **that** is pronounced with the indefinite vowel used for the first syllable of **calamity** (in effect as **th't**), whereas the demonstrative pronoun or adjective is pronounced with the short vowel used for the second syllable of **calamity**; since there is no difference of spelling, what is allowable in speech needs to be avoided in writing. **That** should also not be omitted after less common verbs like **conclude** and **infer**.

It should not, however, be repeated before each clause that it governs, as in **then there is a danger ... that if it were to be elected on a proportional basis that it could claim greater legitimacy** (*The Plant Report* on electoral reform). **That** may be repeated after **and** or **but**, as in **He said that the affair was an outrage and that the chairman should resign**; but when **if** or any other conjunction occurs within the scope of the conjunction **that, that** should occur only once. In the sentence quoted from *The Plant Report*, therefore, the second **that** should be replaced by a comma if it is really meant that the danger consists in the conditional state of affairs. Probably that is not what was meant, so that the better emendation would be **then, if it were to be elected on a proportional basis, there would be a danger that it could claim greater legitimacy**. Whichever was meant, the sentence, as printed, is ungrammatical. (See also *Final Exercises, Exercise 2*.)

Clauses introduced by **whether** usually function as noun-phrases, the only difference being that the corresponding sentence is here an interrogative one. In **I wonder whether the theorem can be proved constructively,** the clause introduced by **whether** is the object of the verb **wonder**, and the corresponding sentence is **Can the theorem be proved constructively?** In **Whether Shakespeare had a hand in the play is a much disputed question**, the clause introduced by **whether** is the subject of the sentence. In the construction **whether ... or not**, however, **whether** often has the sense of 'if', and then the clause does not constitute a noun-phrase; it is only in this case that **whether** may govern something less than a whole clause, as in **The play, whether or not by Shakespeare, is a masterpiece.** Conversely, **if** may substitute for **whether** after a verb like **to ask, to wonder** or **to doubt**, but not in a clause serving as a grammatical subject.

In direct questions, the particles **how, when, where** and **why** are (interrogative) adverbs: **in this manner** and **for that reason** are adverbial phrases, and so **how** and **why**, which mean 'in what manner?' and 'for what reason?', are, grammatically, adverbs; similarly for **when** and **where**. As well as being used to ask direct questions, they can also serve as conjunctions forming indirect question-clauses: in **He asked how it went**, the interrogative sentence corresponding to the clause is of course **How did it go?**

Such a clause again constitutes a noun-phrase, and can be used as a subject as well as an object, for instance in **How he got in is a mystery (It is a mystery how he got in)**, and as a complement of **is**, as in **The outstanding problem is why some people are left-handed.** **How, when** and **where** may also be used as governing an infinitive after a verb like **to know** or **to discover: He did not know how (when, where) to go.** **When** and **where** have multiple uses. They can be used as conjunctions *not* forming a noun-phrase, but of the same kind as **though**, as in **When he arrived, the place was empty** and **Where he bowed, there he fell down dead.** They can also be used as a kind of relative pronoun, as in **the year when the first printed book appeared** and **the place where they laid him.**

Clauses introduced by other conjunctions such as **or, if, because** and **although** do not function in the same way as any type of phrase – noun-phrase or adjectival phrase – not containing a verb. They are simply component sentences in a compound sentence made up of two other sentences; the task of the conjunction is precisely to conjoin two sentences to form a single one. Grammar classifies two clauses joined by **and, but** or **or** as *co-ordinate* clauses, but a clause introduced by **if, because, although**, etc., as a *subordinate* clause, the other being the *main* clause. The distinction has no logical significance, but it has a grammatical one. For instance, in a compound question, verb and subject have to be inverted in the main clause or in both co-ordinate clauses, but not in a subordinate clause: thus **Did he jump or was he pushed?**, but **When you are in Oxford, do you dine in college?**

Once you know what a clause is, you can recognise a conjunction by asking whether it can introduce a clause other than a relative clause (or an indirect-question clause governed by **who, which** or **what**). Conjunctions frequently introduce words or phrases falling far short of forming whole clauses; there is in fact no restriction upon the grammatical character of an expression introduced by most conjunctions. It may be a noun or noun-phrase, as in **he or his brother**, an adjective, as in **poor but honest**, a preposition, as in **to and from**, an adverb, as in **defiantly though nervously**, or any other part of speech.

All that is essential is that the conjunction should connect two expressions of the *same* grammatical character. The phrase **creative and media**, for example, is a solecism, since **creative** is an adjective and **media** a noun. If two pronouns are conjoined, they must be in the same case, nominative or accusative. Why these rules? The underlying idea is that a sentence containing a conjunction not introducing a whole clause is always short for one in which it does so: **He went to and from the station** is short for **He went to the station and he went from the station**.

A logician will object that **Everything is natural or artificial** is not equivalent to **Everything is natural or everything is artificial**; but it *is* equivalent to **It is true of everything that it is natural or it is artificial**, and, in any case, the ideas underlying grammatical constructions need not be logically watertight.

A relative clause can be connected by a conjunction only to another relative clause, and then only by one of the conjunctions **and, but** and **or**. Thus **Peter, devoted to his family and for whom his wife had done so much** must be changed so that the first phrase becomes a relative clause: **Peter, who was devoted to his family and for whom his wife had done so much**. Such a phrase as **Gooch, unable to play in this Test because of illness and who watched his side's resistance end** (J. Thicknesse, *Evening Standard*, 15 February 1993) therefore needs to be emended. One solution in this case would be to take the adjectival phrase into the relative clause: **Gooch who, unable to play in this Test because of illness, watched his side's resistance end.** If **and** is to be kept, that phrase must become part of a relative clause: **Gooch, who was unable to play in this Test ... and who watched ...** But when both relative clauses are introduced by **who**, it is stylistically better to drop the second **who**, thus putting the conjunction inside a single relative clause: **Gooch, who was unable to play in the Test ... and watched ...** Conjunctions like **because** and **although**, which introduce subordinate clauses, *must* be placed inside the relative clause. Thus although **who was poor but who was honest** is properly formed, **who was poor because who was honest** is inadmissible and must be replaced by **who was poor because honest** or **who was poor because she was honest.**

The stylistic principle whereby it is better to drop a second **who** does not apply when both relative pronouns govern the verb **to be: who was poor but who was honest** is more emphatic than **who was poor but honest,** and just as well phrased. The principle does not apply so strongly when both clauses begin with **whom: whom the gods favour and men admire** is not always better than **whom the gods favour and whom men admire.** The principle does apply when both clauses begin with **which,** provided that it is the subject of both. When it is the object of both, the two forms are equally good; but when it is the subject of one and the object of the other, as in **the deer which run wild in the forest and which the King hunts for his pleasure,** it sounds awkward, because faintly ungrammatical, to omit the second **which.** These, however, are niceties: what must *never* be done is to conjoin a relative clause to a phrase like **unable to play.**

As counts as a conjunction, but is frequently an exception to much of the above. In **As they were on their way to the beach, ... ,** it is quite regular: **They were on their way to the beach** is a complete grammatical sentence. In **As I said, ... ,** however, although **I said** is a clause, containing as it does a finite verb, it cannot meaningfully be completed to form a whole sentence. When **as** is used for comparison in the construction **as ... as,** the noun or pronoun following the second **as** must be in the same case as the first term of the comparison, since **as** is a conjunction; the same applies to **than.** Thus it is correct to say **He is not as tall as I,** rather than **He is not as tall as me,** and **He is taller than I,** rather than **He is taller than me.** It is also right to say **She married someone as tall as me, or ... taller than me,** since **someone** is the object of **married; She married**

someone as tall as I or ... **taller than I** is the ungrammatical result of a misplaced attempt to be grammatically scrupulous.

But although, in the first pair of examples, it would be perfectly proper to add a verb, to form **He is not as tall as I am** or **He is taller than I am**, there is no meaningful way to complete the clause **I am** to form one amounting to a whole sentence; and, in the second pair, **She married someone as tall as me/taller than me**, it is not even possible to add a verb. (One can of course say **She married someone as tall as I am** or **She married someone taller than I am**.)

There are other exceptions. The conjunction **whereas** can govern only a whole clause containing a verb. **While**, on the other hand, can govern a mere word or phrase, but does not need to stand between it and another of the same grammatical category. On the contrary, it forms, with an adjective, participle or phrase beginning with a preposition, a kind of adjectival phrase qualifying a noun or noun-phrase. An example is **Odysseus, while asleep, was set ashore at Ithaca** or, equivalently, **Odysseus was set ashore at Ithaca while asleep**; another is **The President, while of a different opinion, applauded the speaker's remarks**. Radio announcers have taken to saying things like **We now continue with our concert, while on Radio 4 an interview with Norman Lamont**. This is of course quite wrong: **while** in such a context must have a verb to govern (**there is** before **an interview**), whereas the announcer is treating it as a kind of preposition.

Some mistakes arising from a misunderstanding of the roles of prepositions and conjunctions are as follows.

And nor, but nor, and neither. **Nor** is already a conjunction, having the sense of 'and ... not ... ', and normally requiring a reversal of order of the subject and verb in the clause it governs: it therefore does not need **and** or **but** to precede it. **And nor** and **but nor** have long been used to lend special emphasis; but recently writers have taken to putting either **and** or **but** before **nor** whenever it occurs, which of course completely destroys the rhetorical effect this pleonasm used to have. It is therefore better always to omit the superfluous **and** and **but**.

But nor, in particular, has become a thorough bore, as in **You can't satirise and name-drop at the same time, but equally, nor can you baptise and name-drop at the same time** (Tom Shone, *Observer*, 7 June 1992), in which the **but** is doing no work at all: **You can't satirise and name-drop at the same time; nor, equally, can you baptise and**

name-drop at the same time conveys the same sense far less clumsily, as does **You can't satirise and name-drop at the same time; but you can't baptise and name-drop at the same time, either.** As for **and neither** (in constructions like **and neither did he return home**), it is completely pointless: it simply means **nor**, by which it should always be replaced.

And moreover, but nevertheless. When **moreover** begins a sentence, or follows a semi-colon, it does not need to be preceded by **and**. The mistake, though less in vogue, is similar to that of writing **and nor**: it was recently the heading of a regular feature in *The Times*. Within a single sentence, **and moreover** is admissible, especially if the two words are separated by a comma, as in **It would be a foolish thing to say, and, moreover, it would cause offence**. It is nevertheless preferable to write **It would be a foolish thing to say; moreover, it would cause offence**. Exactly parallel remarks are to be made about **but nevertheless**, with the addition that, when both words are used, it is better to separate them, as in **I was warned not to go, but I went nevertheless**.

As to. Alice **asked whether** cats eat bats, and then **said that** cats eat bats. In the latter case, she made **the statement that** cats eat bats; but it has become increasingly common to say that, in the former case, she posed **the question as to whether** cats eat bats. The phrase **as to** is here wholly intrusive: it is ugly, it adds nothing to the sense and is in no way needed. It is perfectly in order to speak of **the question whether cats eat bats**; you no more need to insert **as to** in this phrase than to refer to **the statement as to that cats eat bats** or to speak of **asking as to whether cats eat bats**.

> **And shall Trelawney die?**
> **Here's twenty thousand Cornishmen**
> **Will know the reason why.**

If they had demanded to know **the reason as to why**, their roar would have dwindled to a bleat.

The habit of speaking of **the question as to whether** has induced many people always to insert **as to** before **whether** and other interrogative conjunctions like **why**, and thus to say and write **They enquired as to whether** and **They asked as to why**; this is one degree worse than **the question as to why**. A letter in the *Independent* in July 1991 contained the phrase **it is unknown as to whether cannabis was taken**. This is not merely a stylistic mistake, but a definite grammatical one, as may be seen by asking *what* was unknown. The use of **it is** followed by an adjective and then a noun-phrase formed by means of an infinitive is a standard English idiom, equivalent to the result of replacing **it** by the noun-phrase: for example, **It is annoying to lose one's spectacles** is simply an idiomatic way of saying **To lose one's spectacles is annoying**.

In the same way, **It is unknown whether cannabis was taken** is an idiom, equivalent to **Whether cannabis was taken is unknown**; the conjunction **whether** forms a substantival clause which serves as a noun-phrase acting as the subject of **is unknown**. But **as to whether cannabis was taken** is not a noun-phrase, and cannot be the subject of any verb; it is a noun-phrase preceded by a prepositional phrase, meaning 'in relation to whether cannabis was taken'. The writer was therefore saying that something unspecified, related to whether cannabis was taken, is unknown; it can therefore be asked what it *was* that is unknown.

The phrase **as to** is almost always redundant, and is best avoided altogether; on the few occasions when it cannot simply be removed, the substitution of **about** will usually suffice. Writing **the question of whether** is better than writing **the question as to whether**, but is still ugly and pointless: plain English is **the question whether**. In one Finals examination, a candidate felt it necessary to combine the two, writing **the question of as to whether ...**

At and by. **The Chinese economy is growing at the rate of 20% a year** and **The Chinese economy is growing by 20% a year** are both correct; **The Chinese economy is growing at 20% a year** is not.

Different. **Different than** is an Americanism; an extremely convenient one, but still an Americanism. In English as used outside the United States (and possibly Canada), **different** requires **to** or **from** (**from** seems more reasonable, but either is correct): the correct form is **He did it differently from me**, not **He did it differently than I did** or **He did it differently than I** (**He did it differently than me** would be doubly incorrect, since **than** is not a preposition but a conjunction, and requires to be followed by a subject in the same case as the noun or pronoun with which it is contrasted).

Since **to** and **from** are prepositions, they cannot introduce clauses, as **than** can do. This leads to the awkwardness that, where an American can write **that formula had a totally different meaning in Aristotle's mouth ... than it did in Newtonian physics** (H. Putnam), we are tempted into such clumsinesses as **that formula had a totally different meaning in Aristotle's mouth ... from that which it had in Newtonian physics**. Such sentences, though grammatically correct, are better recast, for instance as **that formula had totally different meanings in Aristotle's mouth ... and in Newtonian physics**.

Due to. **Due** is an *adjective*. When it has the sense of 'resulting from', it must of course be followed by the preposition **to**; but it remains an adjective, *not* a prepositional phrase, and must therefore complement or qualify some noun or noun-phrase. It is therefore correct to write **The late arrival of the 10.55 is due to an industrial dispute**, and, equally, **British Rail apologises for the late arrival of the 10.55, due to an industrial dispute**, since, in the first sentence, **due to an industrial dispute** is the complement (after the copula **is**) of the noun-phrase **the late arrival of the 10.55**, and, in the second sentence, it qualifies that noun-phrase. It is incorrect, on the other hand, to write **The 10.55 will be half an hour late, due to an industrial dispute**, because, in this sentence, there is no noun-phrase for **due to an industrial dispute** to complement or qualify. Here **due to** is being wrongly used as a prepositional phrase; the right prepositional phrase to use is **owing to**. The sentence should therefore run **The 10.55 will be half an hour late, owing to an industrial dispute**. This mistake is one of the most common, but should never be made by anyone with aspirations to having a good command of English.

Based on. The mistake about **due to** has long been with us. More recently, a similar mistake about **based on** has become common; sentences like **Based on the Minister's statement, I should not expect an agreement shortly** are frequent in news broadcasts and elsewhere. **Based** is a (verbal) adjective (being a past or passive participle); in a sentence like the above, it is a dangling participle (see 2(d)). The addition of **on** cannot therefore convert it into a prepositional phrase: it must have a noun to qualify. When there is no noun, what is needed is **on the basis of**. An illustration of this (slightly abbreviated from an actual examination script) is **we should not treat others merely based on statistical guidelines based on the group they belong to**. The use of **based on** twice in so short a space (but not in phrases balanced against one another) is a bad defect of style; but a grammatical mistake is involved as well. The second occurrence of **based on** in the sentence is grammatically correct, since **based** there functions as an adjective qualifying **guidelines**. But the first is incorrect, since **based on statistical guidelines** is functioning as an adverbial phrase qualifying **treat others**: **based on** should therefore be replaced by **on the basis of**.

Either ... or; both ... and; not only ... but also. The clauses or phrases connected by **either** and **or**, by **both** and **and** or by **not only** and **but also** or simply **but** should be strictly parallel. **He should either admit or deny that he was wrong, He should either maintain that he was right or admit that he was wrong** and **He should say either that he was right or that he was wrong** are all correct; **He should either say that he was right or that he was wrong** is incorrect, because, since **either** was followed by the infinitive **say, or** should be followed by an infinitive also. Particularly flagrant offenders against this principle are devotees of the split infinitive, who frequently write sentences like **He needs to either revise the chapter or to omit it altogether**.

If the split infinitive is felt to be too precious to lose, the second **to** is superfluous; better, **either** should be placed before the first **to**. An analogous mistake frequently occurs with enumeration; enumerated items ought also to be syntactically parallel. It is wrong to write **The immediate objectives were to (i) curb inflation, (ii) to end the civil war**, or **He argued that (i) the evidence on their side was weak, (ii) that there was strong evidence the other way**. In the second case, either the **that** after **(ii)** should be suppressed, or the **that** before **(i)** should be placed after it; in the first, the **to** before **(i)** should be placed after it.

Except, excepting, including, excluding. **Except** is grammatically anomalous, in that, in addition to its use as a verb, it functions as a preposition and also as a kind of conjunction. It can therefore govern a noun or noun-phrase, as in **They were all present, except the cook**; but it can also govern an adverbial phrase beginning with a preposition, as in **I always wear a tie, except in summer**. When preceded by **not**, **except** must take the form **excepting**: **They were all present, not excepting the cook**; and, when it introduces a whole clause, it must be followed by **that**: **I did very well, except that I never answered more than three questions**. **Including** and **excluding** are participles frequently used as prepositions, as in **Many of the councillors were indicted for corruption, including the Mayor**. In this use, they, unlike **except**, function strictly as *prepositions,* and so cannot be used as governing an adverbial phrase beginning with a preposition. **He swims throughout the year, including in December** is therefore wrong: it should be **He swims throughout the year, including December** or **He swims every month of the year, including December.**

Identical. The preposition following **identical** is **with**, not **to**.

Into. One can **look into** or **enquire into** something; but one **reports on** it, and may then **debate it** or **hold a debate about it.** **A report into the death of seven patients** (BBC TV news, 10 March 1992) should therefore be **A report on the death of seven patients**, while **We don't think that each public enquiry should take the form of a national debate into nuclear** (Cecil Parkinson on *Panorama,* 6 June 1988) should be **We don't think that each public enquiry should take the form of a national debate about nuclear power** (**nuclear** is an adjective, not a noun). (Examples borrowed from J. Ayto, *Observer,* 19 July 1992.)

Just because ... does not mean. It is extremely common to read sentences of the form **Just because we have refused to join the Social Chapter Eleven, shouldn't mean the construction of a British social contract must stop** (*Guardian* leader, 14 December 1991) or **Just because no good argument has been put forward for it does not mean that it is not true.** This is a confusion between **The (mere) fact that no good argument has been put forward for it does not mean that it is not true** and **One should not think, just because no good argument has been put forward for it, that it is not true.**

Like the conjunction **although**, the conjunction **because** is incapable of introducing a substantival clause, that is, one that functions as a noun-phrase, as the word **that** or the phrase **the fact that** can do. The clause introduced by **because** must be attached to a main clause that can stand as a sentence by itself. In **Just because no good argument has been put forward for it does not mean that it is not true**, the main verb **does not mean** has no subject; you can see that a subject is needed if you consider such a sentence as **Just because she lost her temper, they all voted for someone else.** (The comma after **Eleven** in the example from the *Guardian* leader marks a vestigial recognition of the grammatical impropriety.)

If the clause introduced by **Just because** really formed a noun-phrase, no comma would be needed, since it would be the subject of **shouldn't mean**; but if **just because** were used correctly, and the main clause had a proper subject, a comma would indeed be correct. The sentence would be rendered grammatical if **that**, as a demonstrative pronoun, were inserted before **shouldn't**; the insertion of **that**, as a conjunction, after **mean** would also be an improvement.

The reason is because. An indirect question, that is, a clause introduced by **whether, why, how**, etc., is a *substantival clause*. This means that it plays the role of a noun-phrase; in particular, it can follow the verb **to be**, as in **The question is when the discovery was made** and **What I want to know is how you got in**. An indirect *statement* is also a substantival clause; but the only conjunction that can introduce such a clause is **that**. Clauses governed by other conjunctions, such as **although** and **whereas**, cannot be used in this way: as remarked in the preceding entry, this applies also to **because**. Such a sentence as **The reason is because he was jealous** is therefore ungrammatical: it should be **The reason is that he was jealous**. The word **reason** is enough by itself to indicate that the clause gives an answer to a 'Why?' question: there is no need to drive this home by using **because. Because** demands a context like **The reason is unknown, because the correspondence has been lost**, in which the clause it governs explains why the main clause holds good: the loss of the correspondence explains why the reason is unknown. But in the preceding example, the fact that he was jealous does not explain why the reason is: it *is* the reason.

Like, unlike, as, as if. **Like** and **unlike** are adjectives, which can also be used as prepositions which may govern a noun, pronoun or noun-phrase; they cannot govern either a clause or an adverbial phrase. **As**, by contrast, is a conjunction, which can introduce a whole clause or a shorter phrase. It is therefore proper to write **like me** or **unlike me**, but wrong to write **like I am** or **like I do**: it should be **as I am** or **as I do**. For the same reason, **like** should not be used in place of **as if** (which normally requires the subjunctive); **He looked like he was at the end of his tether** should be **He looked as if he were at the end of his tether**. A common mistake is to use **like** or **unlike** as governing an adverb or adverbial phrase, as in **unlike formerly**; examples are **Unlike at the Abdication** and **unlike in those cases** (F. Johnson, *Sunday Telegraph*, 13 and 20 December 1992). The proper replacement for **like** in such contexts is **as**, and, for **unlike**,

not as; but the latter will usually entail recasting the sentence, since a phrase starting **Not as** cannot begin a sentence, and the negative will often better be placed elsewhere, or, if there is already one, omitted. Thus **Unlike at the Abdication, the Press has not concealed the facts** should become **The Press has not, as at the Abdication, concealed the facts**. **The Press has not concealed the facts, as at the Abdication** is equally possible, as is **The Press has not concealed the facts, as it did at the Abdication**; the latter would avert a misunderstanding to which the former might, though should not, give rise. **As at the Abdication, the Press has not concealed the facts** is grammatical, but conveys the unintended sense. Sometimes it will suffice to suppress the preposition after **unlike**: **In prose, unlike in poetry, inversion is rare** is not grammatical; **In prose, unlike poetry, inversion is rare** is.

Out of, off. Americans usually omit the **of** after **out** in phrases like **out the window**, but retain it in ones like **out of order**; probably the distinction concerns whether motion or state is indicated. In British usage, however, **out** is not a preposition, but an adverb; the prepositional phrase before a pronoun or noun-phrase is *always* **out of**. **Off of**, on the other hand, is a crude mistake: **off** *never* admits **of** after it.

Plus. The use of **plus** in place of **and** or **in addition**, though favoured by broadcasters, is a vulgarism and not to be imitated.

That and but that. **There is no question that the accused is guilty** means that the guilt of the accused cannot be seriously entertained. Often phrases of this form are used to mean the opposite. To bear this sense, it is necessary to insert **but**: **There is no question but that the accused is guilty** means that the guilt of the accused cannot be called into question. Conversely, **There is no doubt that the accused is guilty** means that the guilt of the accused cannot be doubted; if **but** were inserted here, it would not yield a sentence clearly meaning the same, or clearly meaning the opposite, but simply one whose meaning was opaque.

The fact that. The use of the word **fact** commits the *speaker* to the truth of the clause following **that**. The sentence **They argue the need for a change of government from the fact that the economy is collapsing** involves an *admission* that the economy is collapsing; to avoid the implication, **from the fact** should be replaced by **on the ground**. Often the implication can be avoided by simply using **that** in place of **the fact that**.

(f) TRANSITIVE AND INTRANSITIVE VERBS

The grammatical distinction between verbs of these two kinds is doubtless familiar to most people; but if any uncertainty about it remains, it is important to dispel it.

A *transitive* verb is one that can be used to form an intelligible sentence only if there is a subject (a noun, pronoun or noun-phrase usually coming before the verb) *and* an object (a noun, pronoun or noun-phrase usually coming after the verb). **To stroke** and **to brush** are both transitive verbs, for example: neither **Cinderella stroked** nor **Cinderella brushed** makes any sense as a sentence on its own, it being necessary to say *what* she stroked or brushed (e.g. **Cinderella stroked the cat** or **Cinderella brushed her hair, the cat** and **her hair** being the objects of the verb in the two sentences respectively).

A few verbs, like **to be, to become** and **to remain** need to be followed, not by an *object*, but by a *complement*. If I say **Mr Jones addressed a city councillor**, you can ask **Which city councillor did Mr Jones address?**, because **address** is a transitive verb, and I was speaking of something Mr Jones did to a particular city councillor. But if I say **Mr Jones remained a bachelor**, it makes no sense for you to ask **Which bachelor did Mr Jones remain?**, because **remain** is an intransitive verb, and my sentence concerns what Mr Jones *was* or *is*. Because in English nouns do not assume different forms in subject and in object position, the distinction between transitive verbs and those that take a complement is only seldom relevant to grammatical form; but it serves to explain why **It was he** is grammatically correct, and **It was him** a slangy colloquialism.

An *intransitive* verb is one like **to sleep** and **to laugh** to which it makes no sense to attach an object. **Cinderella slept** and **Cinderella laughed** are both complete sentences in themselves; it would be nonsense to ask **Cinderella slept** *what?* or **Cinderella laughed** *what?* Note that a transitive verb admits a passive form, in which what would be the object in the straightforward or active form becomes the subject: **the barber cut my hair** becomes **my hair was cut by the barber**. An intransitive verb has no use for a passive form; it makes no sense to say, for example, that something **was rejoiced**, because it makes no sense to say that someone **rejoiced something**. It is equally senseless to say that something **was**

remained. That is why **to be, to become** and **to remain** count as intransitive verbs. Although one could not say just **Mr Jones became** without provoking the question **Mr Jones became** *what?*, one cannot say **A married man was become by Mr Jones** or **A bachelor was remained by Mr Jones**. An intransitive verb often acquires a transitive sense, however, when a preposition is attached to it. Thus, although **to talk** is intransitive, it can be used in the passive in such a context as **I know who is being talked about; to talk about** is here being treated as if it were a single transitive verb, and it would therefore be a great mistake to substitute **whom** for **who**.

Many verbs can be used both transitively and intransitively, for example **to marry** and **to eat; Helen married late in life** means 'Helen married her (first) husband late in life', and **He was eating when I arrived** means 'He was eating some food when I arrived'. It is nevertheless important to know which verbs can be used transitively, which can be used intransitively, and how a given verb is being used in a particular sentence. Some frequent mistakes are listed below.

Prepositional suffixes. English is rich in the use of verbs modified by attaching a preposition used adverbially, such as **to put off, to lay by,** and so forth. It was for this reason that Basic English (a restricted vocabulary for international use) could make do with only twelve verbs: 'to continue' could be expressed by **to go on,** 'to decay' by **to go off,** 'to enter' by **to go into,** etc. Prepositions should not be added to a transitive verb, however, when they do not modify the sense: one should say simply **comprise,** not **comprise of, expound,** not **expound upon, infringe,** not **infringe on,** as in **conditions which infringed on Iraq's sovereignty** (*Independent,* 2 March 1992) and **ponder,** not **ponder on** (as in **pondering on its weaknesses,** G. Baker, *THES,* 7 February 1992).

American English has a horror of transitive verbs, and punishes them by adding *two* prepositional adverbs (more exactly, a prepositional adverb *and* a preposition), as in **meet up with, beat up on** and **miss out on.** This practice (exemplified by **he missed out on Taylor's performance,** letter in the *Guardian,* 17 March 1992) should *not* be imitated: the two prepositions add nothing to the sense of the already transitive verb, but only weaken its impact; **he missed Taylor's performance,** for example, expresses the very same sense. **Put up with** and **look up to,** on the other hand, are firmly entrenched in the British variety of English, and have idiomatic meanings that would not be conveyed by **put** and **look** on their own.

Better. **To better** is a transitive verb, meaning 'to improve' or 'to improve upon'. It cannot be used as an auxiliary verb, like **can** or **must**. My children used often to say things of the form **I better do that, bettern't I?**, which is precisely to treat **better** as an auxiliary verb; I am afraid the mistake is not wholly confined to children. It should be **I had better do that, hadn't I?**: **better** is here an adverb.

Debate. **Kennedy debated Nixon** is an Americanism, to be sedulously avoided. You do not debate your adversary: you debate some subject, such as **the level of taxes, with** your adversary.

Lie and lay. The verb **to lie**, with past tense **lay** and past participle **lain**, is intransitive, and means 'to adopt or maintain a recumbent position' or, with an inanimate subject, 'to be at rest'. The verb **to lay**, with past tense and past participle **laid**, is transitive, and means 'to set down'. To confuse the two is a particularly bad mistake.

Progress. The verb **to progress** is intransitive. One therefore cannot write **have progressed the matter**. Such a verb as **to advance**, which can be transitive or intransitive, is needed instead.

Protest. **To protest** something is to affirm it against those who would deny it, as in **He protested his innocence** or **They protested their right to be present**. To use **protest** with a direct object in the sense of **protest against** is a piece of illiteracy that destroys a useful word.

Research. The *Oxford English Dictionary* gives the use of **to research** as a *transitive* verb as 'rare or obsolete', the latest example it cites being from 1786. It has been revived, and is widely used by television producers to mean 'to assemble a smattering of information, true and false, about'. It is nevertheless better to use the verb only intransitively, speaking of **researching into** Romance philology or whatever it may be.

Rise and raise. **To rise**, with past tense **rose** and past participle **risen**, is an intransitive verb, meaning 'to go up'. **To raise**, with past tense and participle **raised**, is a transitive verb, meaning 'to lift up'.

(g) SINGULAR AND PLURAL

Some writers have lost all sense of the distinction between singular and plural, and use them indiscriminately; besides being offensive to the ear, this is a potent source of ambiguities. A verb must agree in number (singular or plural) with its subject, and a pronoun must agree in number with the noun to which it refers back. Here are two examples from an article in the *Guardian* of 22 November 1991 by Pamela Wells (incorrect plurals italicised):

The ground squirrel may perish, but its altruistic tendencies live on in the bodies of *their* relatives.

... several species have developed altruistic breeding systems in the absense of special genetic systems. The Florida scrub jay *show* some traces of dividing labour in this way.

The same noun-phrase **the ground squirrel** cannot grammatically have both the possessive pronouns **its** and **their** referring back to it, above all not in the same sentence. The subject, **the ground squirrel**, is evidently meant to refer to a species, and not to an individual animal; likewise **the Florida scrub jay** denotes a species, and not an individual bird. Hence **their** should be **its**, and **show** should be **shows**. (Presumably the 'relatives' of the ground squirrel are intended to be several related species; but the use of **their** suggests that they may be individuals of possibly only one other species. If that is the intention, the sentence is thoroughly muddled and should have been recast; in any case, the careless lapse into the plural creates ambiguity. For the misspelling of **absence**, see Section 6.)

Even those who have not abandoned the distinction between singular and plural altogether make frequent mistakes in particular contexts.

A singular subject, even if denoting a group of people, or an organisation involving many people, should be followed by a verb in the singular, and referred back to by a singular pronoun; one thus should write **The Foreign Office was reluctant**, not **were reluctant**, and **The management does not accept responsibility** rather than **do not accept responsibility**. A particularly virulent form of this mistake, constantly committed by the General Board of Oxford University, is the use of an abstract noun such as **staff**, denoting a body with individual members, as a plural noun, as in **the staff who are under the greatest pressure, the academic staff who undertake** and **to some staff**.

Two singular nouns or noun-phrases conjoined by **and** form together a *plural* subject, and must be followed by a verb in the plural, e.g. by **are** rather than **is** when the verb is **to be**. This is easy to overlook when the noun-phrases are long, but should not be overlooked ever. Just before the temporary demise of its Playhouse Theatre, Oxford was disfigured by advertisements, one of which greeted railway travellers as they climbed the stairs of the underpass from platform 2, for a play entitled **Rosencrantz and Guildenstern is Dead**; though increasingly common, this form is inexcusable.

When two nouns or noun-phrases act as subjects connected by **or** or by **nor**, however, the verb should be in the singular if both noun-phrases are, not in the plural as in **a model in which either AC or GCH are false** (M. Tiles, 1989), **that the Song or Ecclesiastes were extremely special texts** and **what Jesus or Paul say**; a pronoun referring back to the disjunctive subject should likewise be in the singular, not in the plural as in **Chemosh or Yahweh might be angry with their worshippers** (the last three examples from R. Lane Fox, 1991). If one noun is singular and the other, connected by **or**, is plural, it will be more elegant to turn the sentence round.

It is often tempting to use a plural verb when the subject is a noun-phrase ending with a plural noun, for instance **the exchange rate of these currencies**; but it is the number of the *main* noun (here **exchange rate**) that counts. A more complex example is **liquidation of the crucial remnants of a theocratic state are a vital precondition of Unionist trust** (Hugo Young, *Guardian*, 25 February 1992): the subject is **liquidation** and the verb should therefore be **is**. One that jars particularly badly is **To claim that such restrictions inconvenience the elderly and disabled disproportionately are untrue** (letter in the *Independent*, 16 July 1992): the subject is **to claim** and the verb should again be **is**. The rule applies to such phrases as **a group of prisoners** and **a section of Conservative MPs**. When the main noun is itself **number**, however, it is pedantic to make the verb singular, as in **A number of MPs is discontented**; **A number of MPs are discontented** is the natural thing to say. In the view of many, but by no means of all, the same applies to **majority** and **minority**.

The converse mistake is exemplified by **the application of general characteristics to those to whom it may not be applicable**. Here the singular pronoun **it** has been used because the main noun in **the application of general characteristics** is singular, but inappropriately: the pronoun should be **they**, because it is the general characteristics that are applied, not their application. This illustrates the need to attend to sense, rather than following grammatical rules blindly.

Some particular mistakes about singular and plural forms are as follows.

Neither ... nor; both ... and. In a phrase like **neither the first nor the second speaker**, the noun should be in the singular, it being understood after **first**; and the same applies to **both the first and the second speaker**.

Behaviour. Nouns referring to material objects or substances are of two kinds: those like **tree** which admit of a plural and of the indefinite article (**trees, a tree**), and those like **mud** which do not (**muds** can be used only to mean 'kinds of mud'). Those of the former kind are known as 'count-nouns'; those of the latter as 'mass-terms'. Mass-terms, like count-nouns, can be prefixed by **the** and **some**; unlike them, they allow of partitive constructions (**a patch of mud, a pint of beer, a glass of water, a bar of gold**), as well as being able to stand on their own without an article. What is less often clearly grasped is that precisely the same distinction applies to abstract nouns. **Action** is a count-noun, admitting **an action** and **actions**; **behaviour** is the abstract equivalent of a mass-term. If one wants to refer to how several people behave, one must therefore say **Their behaviour is offensive**, since **behaviour** neither admits nor needs a plural. Likewise, **behaviour** will not admit the indefinite article. One may say **That was impeccable behaviour**; but, if the indefinite article **a** is felt to be needed, a partitive construction must be used – **That was an impeccable piece of behaviour**. Admittedly, sociologists and psychologists have for some years been treating **behaviour** as a count-noun, speaking of **behaviours** and of **a behaviour**. Those who are not engaged with these subjects should not imitate their example; nor, indeed, should those who are.

Greek, Latin and Italian plurals. **Phenomena, criteria, data, media** and **strata** are all (neuter) *plural* nouns, the first two Greek, the other three Latin: the singulars are **phenomenon, criterion, datum, medium** and **stratum**. Plurals with **-s** have never been used with these nouns; only the Greek and Latin plurals with **-a**. It is therefore ungrammatical to say or write **that phenomena, a criteria, this data, the media is** or **a strata;**

the correct forms are **that phenomenon, a criterion, these data, the media are** and **a stratum**. It is important to continue to treat these words as plurals, because we sometimes need the singular, as in **Television is the wrong medium for explaining scientific theories.**

The confusion arises because in Latin and Greek a noun ending in **-a** may be either a neuter plural, whose singular would generally be **-um** in Latin or **-on** in Greek, or a feminine singular, whose plural in Latin would be **-ae**.

The Latin word **insignia** has also been taken into the language, and is also plural, but its singular form **insigne** does not exist in English; it should nevertheless be used as a plural. The same applies to **graffiti**, which English has borrowed from Italian, whereas it sounds somewhat affected to employ its (masculine) singular form **graffito**, which has not been taken into the language; but respect for the language from which **graffiti** originates should inhibit its use as a singular noun, as in **the graffiti is** or **a graffiti**. **Agenda** (Latin for 'things to be done') is also, properly speaking, plural, but its treatment as such would sound preposterously pedantic; a purist may find **an agenda** and **agendas** grate upon his ear, but since we never use the singular **agendum**, they should certainly be allowed.

A plural Latin noun that has definitely become a singular English one is **stamina**; but, then, its singular **stamen** has acquired a completely different meaning, whereas **phenomenon, datum**, etc., are likely to die if their plurals come to be treated as singular. Do not be misled, however, into supposing **flora** and **fauna** to be plural forms: they are *singular* collective nouns.

Sort of, kind of. Trollope was addicted to phrases of the form **those sort of people**, as if **sort of** were a composite adjective. It is not, however: **sort** retains the character of a noun. **That sort of person** is therefore perfectly correct. **That sort of people** is *grammatically* correct, but has a clumsy sound. **Those sorts of people** is of course unobjectionable on any count, but it should not be used if only a single sort is in fact in question. In that case, it is better to say **people of that sort**. To use **sort of** to qualify a verb, adjective or adverb, as in **He sort of slumped in his chair** and **She looked sort of irritated**, is inexcusable. All this applies equally to **kind of.**

(h) NUMBER AND QUANTITY

Less and fewer. **More** has two inverses: **less** and **fewer**; they should not be confused. **Less** relates to amount, **fewer** to number, that is, to *cardinal* number: one should thus say **There is less salt in this dish than in that,** but **There are fewer salt-cellars on this table than on that.** Cardinal numbers answer a question beginning 'How many ... ?', rather than one of the form, 'How much?', 'How long?', 'How big?', etc. More precisely, they occur when what is in question is how many things there are of a certain kind (e.g. people) of each of which something holds good (e.g. that he or she is in this room).

Thus, when you ask **How many miles to Babylon?**, you are *not* asking for a cardinal number, but how far it is in miles to Babylon; the answer **Less than a thousand** is therefore grammatically correct, whereas, if you had asked **How many wise men live in Babylon?**, the answer should be *Fewer* **than a thousand.** You can easily tell whether a number is a cardinal number or not by asking yourself whether only a whole number would make sense; if **five and a quarter** would make sense, the number is *not* a cardinal number but a measurement-number: you can be five and a quarter miles from Babylon, but there could not be five and a quarter wise men there. An important elementary distinction in the foundations of mathematics is thus reflected in English grammar. This is one case in which a victory, over supermarket chains, has recently been scored by those resisting linguistic pollution.

Majority. What is wrong with **The majority of the houses were destroyed**? A purist would replace the plural form **were** by **was**, on the ground that **majority** is a singular noun; the point is contentious, but I should regard the emendation as pedantic, since we are merely concerned with *number*. **The majority of the town was destroyed,** on the other hand, is definitely ungrammatical, since **majority** does *not* mean 'the greater part', but 'the greater number': **the greater part** should be used instead. The real objection to **The majority of the houses were destroyed,** on the other hand, is stylistic, not grammatical: when there is no particular point in using **the majority** or **the greater part,** the simple word **most** is more forceful and should always be preferred. Better, therefore, would be **Most of the houses were destroyed** and **Most of the town was destroyed**; note that **most** is plural in the first of these sentences and singular in the second, because in the first it concerns number and in the second quantity.

One of. When **one of** is followed by a list, the last two items of the list should be joined by **and**, not by **or**: **Discuss with reference to *one* of Caesar, Pompey and Crassus**, not *one* **of Caesar, Pompey or Crassus.**

(i) FUTURE AND CONDITIONAL

The principle long accepted is that the ordinary future requires **shall** in the first person (singular and plural) and **will** in the second and third persons; likewise, the conditional requires **should** in the first person, and **would** in the second and third. **Will** in the first person, and **shall** in the second or third, therefore give a special emphasis, usually indicating intention on the part of the speaker, as in **They shall not pass.** The story that used to be used by schoolteachers as a mnemonic for this is that of the foreigner who fell into the river and cried **I will drown, and nobody shall save me!**; he drowned because the bystanders understood him as determined to do so.

The Authorised Version contains many uses of **shall** in the third person that do not indicate intention on the writer's part, as in **He shall feed his flock**; but that is archaic, and should not be imitated. In reported speech, when the main verb is in the past tense, **should** and **would** represent the original speaker's use of the ordinary future tense, as in **He said that he would be retiring next year**; but whether **should** or **would** is used depends upon whether the subject of the current sentence is in the first or in the second or third person, *not* the subject of the reported sentence. In this case, what the original speaker said was **I shall be retiring next year.** Contrast **She said that I should live to regret it**, where the words she used were **You will live to regret it.** **Should** of course also has the sense of **ought to.** It may cause confusion to use it in this sense in the first person; it is safer to use **ought to** in this instance.

There are other uses of **will** and **would** than to form the future tense and the conditional mood. Thus **will** is also used, in the first person as well as in the second and third, in the sense of 'have a will to', for instance in **not as I will, but as thou wilt.** In an extension of this sense it is applied to inanimate objects, as in **The car won't start.** When so used, **would** is its past tense: **Though they pressed me, I would not consent. Will** also sometimes has the sense of 'habitually', as in **He *will* address me as 'Sir'**;

would is again its past tense, as in **We would talk for hours about our plans for the future**. With no connotation of past time, **would** can be used in the sense of 'long to', as in **the haven where I would be**.

(j) SUBJUNCTIVES

There *is* a subjunctive mood in English, with present, imperfect and perfect tenses, though it keeps what is called a low profile. It is probably its low profile that causes almost all Germans, when speaking English, to put the verb of the antecedent of a conditional sentence into the conditional mood, saying things like **If I would apply, they would accept me**, although in fact the true English construction is exactly analogous to the German one. In all three tenses of the subjunctive, the verb has the same form in all three persons, singular and plural. In the present tense, it has the same form as the infinitive (without **to**). It is chiefly used in clauses giving the content of orders, conditions and demands, as in: **He demanded that the council recognise his rights; on condition that she refrain from criticising the Department in public or in private;** and **He asked that I be quiet**.

The imperfect tense has the same form as the third person plural of the imperfect indicative, and is used in conditionals referring to present time but with improbable or impossible antecedents, like **If I were an Indian citizen, I should support Congress** and **If I went to China, ...** ; as in other Indo-European languages, the verb of the consequent assumes the conditional mood. Save when the verb is **to be** or **to have**, the construction **were to ...** is often used instead: **If I were to go to China, ...** In everyday speech, **was** is often substituted for **were** in such contexts; this is much better avoided in writing or formal speech.

The perfect subjunctive is formed by **had** and the past participle, and is answered by a perfect conditional in the consequent: **If I had gone to Italy, I should never have met you**. The reference to past time is often very faint, so that it is permissible to say **if I had now been in Rome**; but the antecedent is definitely being presented as stating a condition known to be false. Imperfect and perfect subjunctives are also used after **as if**, with the verb of the main clause in the indicative.

(k) Concluding remark about Latin

Opponents of the use of the classics in education have allied themselves with those who wish to deny or play down what have traditionally been taken to be rules of English grammar in maintaining that grammarians have in the past formulated those rules by false analogy with Latin: this thesis has come to be so frequently stated, without illustration or serious examination, as to have attained the status of a dogma. In one respect it is quite obviously false. Latin is a highly inflected language. It can therefore rely on the termination of a noun, adjective or verb to indicate its role in the sentence, and can accordingly be extremely lax about word-order, which can be varied for rhetorical or rhythmic effect without impropriety and without perplexing the reader. A striking example is the ending of a collect in the Roman Missal: ... **nos inducat in omnem, sicut tuus promisit Filius, veritatem**. This means 'may lead us into all truth, as your Son has promised'; but the word-order is 'us may-lead into all, as your has-promised Son, truth'. Little of the kind may be done in English, because, being a largely uninflected language, the role of a word in a sentence is primarily indicated by its position; the rules governing the order of words in an English sentence are subtle. Nothing corresponds to them in Latin, and nobody has ever maintained that it does.

A second consequence of this primary difference is that the use of auxiliary verbs is very restricted in Latin, and very extensive in English. We form the future tense with **will** and **shall**, the perfect tense with **has** or **have**, the pluperfect with **had**, the conditional with **would** or **should**, the passive with **am, is, are, was, were** or **will be**, and even the present tense with **am, is** or **are** when the sense is continuous, or with **do** or **does** in interrogative or negative sentences, and we usually form our infinitives with **to**; in all these cases a single word – an inflected form of the verb (i.e. of what in English would be the main verb) – will suffice in Latin, while the Latin subjunctive is often to be rendered by **may** or **should**.

In these two ways, Latin grammar is extremely different from English, and no one has ever pretended otherwise. Where the two grammars *are* similar is in the classification of the different roles that words can play in sentences: the 'parts of speech', the cases of nouns, the tenses and moods of verbs. Even here there are marked differences – Latin has no articles and no continuous tenses, English has no dative or ablative case, using prepositions instead. Nevertheless, the similarity, due to the fact that Latin and English belong to the same Indo-European family of languages, is far-reaching enough for much of the grammatical terminology of the one to be transferable to the other: the distinctions between adjective and adverb, between noun and adjective, between transitive and intransitive verbs, between active and passive, between nominative and accusative, and many more. The advantage claimed by proponents of the teaching of Latin, that it improves the students' mastery of *English* grammar, rests on the fact that, in learning Latin, this terminology, and a grasp of the distinctions it draws, is essential, since one cannot otherwise learn the inflections for case, tense and mood, whereas a native speaker of English may never appreciate the need for them. We need not decide this educational point here; but when you are told, for the thirtieth time, that alleged grammatical rules of English are all based on false analogies with Latin, you should insist on being told in what respect, and consider whether the analogy is false or not, and whether, if false, it has ever been claimed.

3. Some Stylistic Maxims

The fundamental rule of writing is that the writer should pay attention to his words, so as to leave the reader free to concentrate on the thoughts expressed. Your reader ought never to have to pause to consider what thought *is* being expressed; if he does, you have failed as a writer. To avoid this effect requires a vivid awareness, in writing, of the words and constructions you are using: *you* must think consciously of the words you are using, so that the reader does not need to. Under pressure, as in an examination, you have little attention to spare for the words, rather than their content; that is why you need to cultivate the habit of attending to them as much as to the content (and each in relation to the other), so that clear expression becomes as nearly automatic as possible.

The sentences of a great stylist will be noted and admired. Few of us can aspire to that; our object should be to make our writing unobtrusive, so that its sense can be immediately apprehended and the reader is never distracted from it.

(a) The principle has three corollaries. The first is, of course, to take care to say what you mean. You must cultivate the habit of asking yourself what your sentences say, as you compose them, and whether that is what you meant. If, for example, you have written **house prices and debt levels reached unsustainably high levels** (W. Hutton, *Guardian*, 17 December 1991), you should consider how a level çan reach a level. Obviously it cannot: a level stays where it is, while other things reach it or fall short of it. You should not then say to yourself, 'Everybody will know what I mean, namely that the *debts* reached unsustainably high levels'. Certainly, in this case, the readers will know what you meant. They may even have become so habituated to this sort of writing that they will not consciously notice that what you wrote is nonsense. That does not justify you in shrugging your shoulders: you should take the trouble to cross out **debt levels** and substitute **debts**. For otherwise the fact that you have not bothered to say what you mean makes the sentence disagreeable to read, whether or not the absurdity is consciously noticed.

If you fail to say what you mean, one of two things will happen. You may simply be misunderstood. Or what you have actually said may be so absurd or irrelevant that the reader recognises at once that you could not have meant *that*; he then has to guess at what you did intend. In a case like that just cited, this presents no difficulty. Often, however, the reader may have to puzzle over your meaning. Even if he is able to guess it very swiftly, he may sometimes do so wrongly; and when he does guess it correctly, he may have been held up, and his attention diverted from thinking about the truth of what you were aiming to say.

(b) The second corollary is that, for similar reasons, you should avoid ambiguity. This is often difficult to do: if your mind is exclusively on the thoughts you are expressing, you may easily not notice that a sentence you have written could be taken another way. This again illustrates the need, when not writing under pressure, for having the words, as well as the thought, at the forefront of your mind.

Even when it is quite obvious what you mean, the presence of an unintended meaning may make your mode of expression ridiculous. Only inattention to the words being used can explain an organisation's being named the **Association of Secondary Heads**, for example, with the macabre suggestion of subsidiary heads growing out of people's shoulders as in Walter Miller's *A Canticle for Leibowitz*.

There are ambiguities of words, like this, and ambiguities of construction. Many sentences of English, as of any language, are structurally ambiguous, as far as grammar goes. Often, the alternative sense is so obviously unintended that the reader does not even notice it. Nevertheless, although he may not even be conscious of it, the slight effort he has made in order to construe the sentence as it was meant is the source of an impression he receives of roughness of style. Even ambiguities that will mislead no one are therefore to be avoided.

A simple example of an ambiguity of construction is **The New Commonwealth of Independent States ... will be up and running and replace the old Soviet Union in a month's time** (P. Pringle, *Independent*, 17 December 1991). This is by no means such a terrible sentence as some quoted in this book, but it *is* ambiguous: there is nothing to show whether **in a month's time** is intended to qualify only **will ... replace the old Soviet Union** or also **will be up and running**. The ambiguity here caused by the careless placing of the adverbial phrase is unimportant, because **will be up and running** is so vague an expression; but it would have impaired the writer's endeavour to communicate with his readers if he had been saying anything more precise.

Furthermore, the successive uses of **and** are momentarily confusing: after the second of them, the reader is expecting something parallel with the words **up** and **running**, whereas the second **and** actually connects **be up and running** with **replace the old Soviet Union**. It would be kinder to the reader to put a comma after **running**, or, better, to repeat **will** before **replace**. Thus the sentence would be better recast **In a month's time, the New Commonwealth of Independent States ... will be up and running and will replace the old Soviet Union** if **in a month's time** was meant to qualify both verb-phrases (predicates), or **The New Commonwealth of Independent States ... will be up and running and will, in a month's time, replace the old Soviet Union** if it was meant to qualify only the second of the two.

(c) The third corollary is that the structure of your sentences should never surprise the reader. It is easy, if you are not attending to *how* you have expressed yourself, to compose a sentence that, up to a certain point, leads the reader to expect it to have a structure which, at that point, he discovers that it cannot have. Sometimes he will have to go back to the beginning and read the whole sentence again; even when he does not, his attention will, once more, have been diverted from the thought to the words. A simple example, again taken from the *Guardian*, is: **Taxed recently about this, he said that style was now rather out of fashion.** Having arrived at the end of the sentence, the reader, puzzled by the exceptional fatuity of the remark, will look again; he will then realise that **that** was not a conjunction but a demonstrative adjective. If the journalist had written, **Taxed recently about this, he said that that style was now rather out of fashion**, the irritation would not have occurred. Several of the maxims stated below follow from this corollary.

Another example of a sentence liable to cause the reader at least momentary perplexity is the following, from an article by Melanie Phillips in the *Guardian* for 22 November 1991: **Yet it is also a fact that staying on rates are shooting up, so GCSE seems to be having some success in encouraging pupils to stay on at school.** When he reaches the word **staying**, a reader may very well take it as a gerund; he will be unsure which rates people are supposed to be staying on, but will expect to be enlightened as he reads further. The plural verb **are** will then show him that he has probably misunderstood (though if he has previously read the article by Pamela Wells in the same issue, quoted under 2(g), he will not be sure). The effect could have been avoided simply by inserting a hyphen in **staying-on**; alternatively, by inverting the two clauses: **Yet GCSE seems to be having some success in encouraging pupils to stay on at school, in view of the fact that staying on rates are shooting up.** Although a hyphen is still needed here, its absence causes no ambiguity because the relevant sense of **staying on** has already been indicated.

Apart from its slangy use of **rate** to mean 'proportion', and the pointless plural **rates**, the original sentence, of 29 words, also well exemplifies clumsy construction, with its unnecessary repetition. One more agreeable to read, of only 20 words, would be: **Yet GCSE may be encouraging pupils to stay on at school, the proportion of those doing so having risen steeply.**

Repetition is sometimes useful for rhythmic or rhetorical effect: **just the worst time of year for a journey, and such a long journey.** When no such effect is aimed at, it is irritating and should be avoided by means of one of the many devices language affords for the purpose.

(d) A number of particular errors of style are now listed.

Clichés. It is universally acknowledged that clichés such as **take on board, at the end of the day, the bottom line, quantum leap, a wide range of issues, key player, put on hold, state of the art, a different ball-game, cutting edge, come out of the closet, put on the back burner, conventional wisdom** and **fundamentally** (or **deeply**) **flawed** are to be avoided: they are irritating and suggest processes of thought that run in pre-existing grooves. Yet worse examples are **when it comes to the crunch, the nitty-gritty** and **at this point in time; at this moment in time** is not only a cliché, but a pleonasm, since **moment** already means 'point in time'.

The maxim that one should avoid clichés is not easily followed; but the effort to express oneself in fresh words is often rewarding. It is necessary to cultivate a sensitivity to hackneyed phrases. An agreeable way of doing so is to read P. G. Wodehouse with attention to his use of language. Bertie Wooster, for instance, never employs clichés inadvertently; he uses them for jocular effect, but always flags them **(I went with what are known as leaden feet; The situation was what is called fraught with peril).**

The word **parameters** is a particular snare: not only has it become a cliché, but it is usually used inaccurately.

Parameters are variables in a mathematical equation or formula which, in specific applications, become constants when assigned definite values. Metaphorical uses of the word **parameter** should be consistent with its literal meaning; but they are best avoided altogether.

Another obnoxious cliché is **trying to tell us something**. The phrase should be used only when there is a genuine obstacle to communication, not due to the obtuseness of the person communicated with, which the communicator has only imperfectly overcome. The Mother Superior of a convent in financial difficulties after being fined for keeping chickens in inhumane conditions remarked, "I think God is trying to tell us something". God cannot be thought to be making an ineffectual attempt to convey a message; he was either telling the nuns something or he was not. Phrases like **what Shakespeare was trying to tell us** are absurd for a comparable, if less compelling, reason.

I and we. The so-called 'editorial' **we** should be avoided. There is some excuse for an *editor's* using the plural form, because he is speaking on behalf of a whole editorial body; but what is usually called an 'editorial' **we** is actually an *authorial* **we**, and there is no excuse for a single writer's giving himself such airs: in doing so, he makes himself look pompous or ridiculous or both. On the whole, one should avoid referring to oneself if possible when not engaged in autobiography. Sometimes, however, a writer is unable to avoid mentioning himself personally; he should then do so boldly, using the pronoun **I**, rather than in some evasive manner. The use of **we** in a genuinely plural sense is of course quite legitimate; but care is needed.

Malay, very usefully, has two first-person plural pronouns, **kita** for when the group it refers to includes the person or people addressed, and **kami** for when it excludes them. A writer is of course addressing his readers, and he should take care to use **we** only in the sense of **kita**, *never* of **kami**. Thus you should avoid assuming that 'we' are white, or Christians, or Protestants (or of Christian or Protestant upbringing), except, of course, when you are explicitly addressing an exclusively white, Christian or Protestant readership. It is easy to make such assumptions inadvertently; a writer needs to notice what his sentences containing **we** imply.

Inappropriate metaphors. Improper metaphors arise from applying an expression intended in a metaphorical sense to things of the very kind from which the metaphor is taken. Among examples I have actually heard are **Two football teams have a common goal** and **Those two houses are not in the same street**; in the first, the common goal was taken to be winning, and, in the second, the architectural merits of the houses were being compared. The result, whether literally true or false, is invariably ludicrous.

Mixed metaphors. Being conscious of the literal meaning of any phrase one uses metaphorically helps one to think of fruitful elaborations of the metaphor; it also protects one from the ludicrous results of mixing metaphors, as in **the prospects of reform had fallen at the first hurdle** (R. Gott, *Guardian*, 23 November 1991), **the tangled web of fraud that has dogged the bank's operations** (Channel 4 News) or **The deep rift that had never healed between Parry and Ernest Gambier Parry came home to roost in November** (J. Dibble, 1992, quoted by A. Porter).

Literally. The adverb **literally** of course means 'in a strict, untransferred, non-metaphorical sense'. It should *never* be used non-literally for mere emphasis. The result of doing so is usually comic, as when a former member of an Oxford college wrote in a letter to its present head, **Since my retirement, I have literally buried myself in my garden**.

In terms of. Those easily influenced by linguistic fashions should beware of one rife amongst broadcasters and military and governmental spokesmen: the use of **in terms of** to avoid having to think how to construct their sentences, or even what precisely they mean. This must represent the lowest point so far in the current degradation of the English language.

Thus they utter sentences like **We have made great progress in terms of the balance of payments**, meaning 'The balance of payments has improved', and **Our troops have been highly successful in terms of advancing into enemy territory**, meaning 'Our troops have advanced deep into enemy territory', **They have been dabbling in secondary banks in terms of investment** (Channel 4 News), meaning 'They have been investing in secondary banks', **very great pressure across the University in terms of teaching load is being felt by ... lecturers** (General Board of Oxford University), meaning 'lecturers throughout the University are bearing very heavy teaching loads', and others that resist interpretation. **In terms of** is rightly used only to state by what means something is, or is to be, specified: on what basis an expression is defined, in what units a measurement is given, or the like.

Parallel phrases. When two phrases are parallel, it is usually better not to write the second in full. **Seventy Labour MPs have declared themselves in favour of the amendment, and twenty-five Labour MPs have declared themselves against the amendment** is pointlessly wordy: **Seventy Labour MPs have declared themselves in favour of the amendment, and twenty-five against it** is clearer and more pleasant to read. Likewise, in **they are related to Goodman's irrealism on the one hand, and to Saussure's doctrine of incommensurability, on the other hand**, the second occurrence of **hand** is quite redundant: **they are related to Goodman's irrealism on the one hand, and to Saussure's doctrine of incommensurability, on the other** is more elegant and quite unambiguous.

When a comparison is made, the conjunction **than** or **as** will necessarily relate two parallel phrases. It is again usually better to leave part of the first to be understood or to be expressed by a pronoun than to repeat it; but it is advisable to make an exception for a preposition. **He owed less to judgement than luck** is scarcely ambiguous; no one is likely to take it to mean **He owed less to judgement than luck did**. Nevertheless, the fact that, grammatically, it could mean that has the unconscious effect of making **He owed less to judgement than to luck** sound better. Omission of the preposition becomes a more serious stylistic fault when it leaves it less than immediately clear to how much of the first phrase the second is to be taken as parallel. An example is **were more the product of Welsh student politics than responsible reflection** (M. Symonds, *Independent*, 16 July 1992). What is meant, of course, is 'were more the product of Welsh student politics than they were the product of responsible reflection', not 'were more the product of Welsh student politics than they were responsible reflection'. To repeat **were ... the product** would be ungainly and pointless, and they are quite rightly left to be understood. It is, however, a mistake of style – though not, properly speaking, of grammar – to omit the **of** before **responsible reflection**: the sentence would read more elegantly if it were inserted, because that would remove a structural ambiguity. We do not consciously notice the ambiguity, since the alternative sense is so obviously unintended; but the slight effort we need to construe the sentence is what gives the impression of stylistic awkwardness.

Parentheses between adjectives and nouns. There is a growing tendency to insert a parenthetical phrase, enclosed by commas or in brackets, between an adjective and the noun it qualifies: a good example is **these simple (but of such resonance among his followers) ideas** (K. Botsford, *Independent*, 12 October 1992). The tendency is to be stoutly resisted; written and spoken language ought not to diverge so widely. The practice is a partial imitation of German (a complete imitation would run **these simple but among his followers so resonant ideas**); such constructions are quite unnatural in English. They can be easily avoided: **these simple ideas, of such resonance among his followers,** and **these ideas, simple but of such resonance among his followers,** are far smoother and less clumsy.

Situation, basically, facility. Some fashions in words endure, others prove transitory. For example, that for adding **situation** to as many nouns as possible (**in a war situation** for **at war, in a travel situation** for **while travelling,** etc.) has fortunately passed without leaving a remnant; possibly it received its coup de grâce when a Trade Unionist declared on television **This is a cock-up situation**. The latest multi-purpose noun is **facility**; military spokesmen in the Gulf War spoke of a mosque as a **religious facility,** and of Ur of the Chaldees as an **archaeological facility**. During the 1970s, a whole phalanx of political activists, wont to begin every utterance with **Well, er, basically, ...,** threatened to empty the word **basically** of all content. The vogue for this profligate use of **basically** is now ebbing; it may go the way of **situation. Basically** has in fact a quite definite meaning, namely 'fundamentally' or 'at the deepest level'. It should be used only when a contrast is being drawn, or is at least implicit, with what appears superficially or holds good at some higher level.

-related. Like the nouns **situation** and **facility** and the phrase **in terms of,** the suffix **-related** is among the modern devices for avoiding the trouble of saying precisely what one means. It is even vaguer than the lexicographer's **of or pertaining to,** having no more definite sense than 'having some connection or other with'; thus a drug-related offence can be one involving the sale or distribution of drugs, one prompted by the desire to obtain drugs, or one committed under the influence of drugs.

Moreover, the suffix is attached, not only to a noun, as in **alcohol-related disease**, but also to an adjective, as in **academic and academic-related staff**, the unlovely piece of jargon regularly used in official communications by the General Board of Oxford University, the UFC, etc. **Alcohol-related disease** is at least grammatical, meaning 'disease related to alcohol'; but **academic-related staff** can be construed only as 'staff related to academic', which violates grammar and makes no sense. To employ this inelegant termination is to demonstrate unwillingness to think of the words to express one's meaning: if you find yourself using it, cross it out at once and consider what you do mean.

Nouns as verbs. Although English contains many words capable of being used both as nouns and as verbs (e.g. **attack, copy, water**), the effect of wantonly increasing their number by using as a verb a word hitherto known only as a noun, when a perfectly good verb already exists, is almost always ugly. An especially hideous example is the use of the verb **to author**; another is **to impact** (instead of **to impinge on**). In other cases, there is no already existing verb, but only a phrase: **to parent**, used intransitively for **to bring up children; to guest**, for **to appear as a guest star**; and **to party**, for **to attend** (or **give**) **a party**. To my ear, these additions to the language are all unattractive.

Noun on noun. German delights in forming compound nouns by piling one noun upon another. Thus a method of proof is **eine Beweismethode**, and a proof of underivability is **ein Unableitbarkeitsbeweis**: a method of proving underivability is, naturally, **eine Unableitbarkeitsbeweismethode**. German and English are different languages, with different inclinations in many matters, including the formation of compound noun phrases. There is no good reason to imitate German by forming such phrases in a similar way: **proof of underivability** is much better than **underivability proof, method of proof** much better than **proof-method** and **method of proving underivability** almost infinitely better than **underivability proof method**.

Likewise, the phrase **knowledge ascription intuitions**, taken from an article published in a philosophical journal, would be much better replaced by **intuitions about ascribing knowledge**. Those who, entranced by the German construction, cannot forbear to use it in English, too, would do better to go the whole hog, writing **underivabilityproofmethod, knowledgeascriptionintuitions** and so forth, or at least **underivability-proof-**

method and **knowledge-ascription-intuitions**. They would thus save the reader from coming up with a jerk when he realises that the noun he had taken to be functioning as a noun is in fact functioning as an adjective; but there is really no justification for copying German in this respect at all.

English is rich in compounds consisting of a noun preceded by a participle, such as **dining room, bathing dress, sailing boat, riding habit, playing card, winning post, paving stone**, etc. A very recent tendency, which should be stoutly resisted, is to substitute a noun (or verb in the infinitive) for the participle, as in the abominable **start date** (**starting date** is of course a perfectly acceptable member of the class just mentioned). It is a puzzle that some English people should be keen on phrases that sound like blunders of a foreigner, because contrary to the principles of formation that have given the language its flavour.

Ongoing. There is nothing wrong with the word **ongoing**, save that it has been so overused in the past fifteen years as to demonstrate that a single word can become a cliché. Try **continuing** or **current** instead.

Only. The word **only** is best placed before the word it qualifies; other positions can generate ambiguity. **He spoke only to Ney** implies that he spoke to no one else; **He only spoke to Ney** might mean that he gave him no written message. When the rhythm of a sentence would be spoiled by strict adherence to this precept, it need not be slavishly followed. An example is Gibbon's misplaced **only**, when, writing of the trial of the anti-Pope John XXIII, he says: **The most scandalous charges were suppressed; the vicar of Christ was only accused of piracy, murder, rape, sodomy, and incest.**

Or whatever. The expression **or whatever** is a slang abbreviation of **or whatever it may be**; like all slang, it should be avoided in writing. **Or the like** is an acceptable substitute.

Here are two cases of misused quotations:
(1) *More honoured in the breach*. The familiar phrase from *Hamlet*, **more honoured in the breach than in the observance**, applied to some practice, is often misused to mean that it is more usual to neglect than to observe it; it actually means that it is more honourable to neglect it than to observe it.

(2) *Breaking the mould*. The sole lasting accomplishment of the now defunct Social Democratic Party seems to have been to induce everyone to misuse the tag **breaking the mould**. It comes from Ariosto's *Orlando Furioso*, in which the poet says of the Scottish hero Zerbino that **Nature made him, and then broke the mould (Natura il fece, e poi roppe la stampa)**, so that she could never make his like again. To break the mould is therefore, in general, a deplorable, not an admirable, thing to do.

Quote. **Quote** is a verb; the corresponding noun is **quotation**. The use of **quote** as a noun is a piece of American slang, not admissible in writing. Would you not be surprised to see *The Oxford Dictionary of Quotes* for sale in Blackwell's bookshop?

Single. A phrase like **the one single mistake she made** is a pleonasm. You cannot make two single mistakes: if there are two of them, they are not single. **The one mistake, the sole mistake** and **the single mistake** all have the same sense. Properly speaking, **the single most dangerous step he could have taken** and **the one most dangerous step he could have taken** are also pleonasms. **The most dangerous step he could have taken** denotes that step which was more dangerous than any other he could have taken; logic rules out there being more than one such. It may be retorted that one may with propriety speak of **the two most dangerous steps he could have taken**. This certainly provides some excuse for **the one most dangerous**: the speaker wishes to emphasise that he is not talking of the two or more most dangerous steps. Nevertheless, a step that is one of the two most dangerous cannot be inferred to be *the* most dangerous; so **the most dangerous step**, in the singular, still unambiguously refers to a determinate one, and the insertion of **single** or **one** before **most**, while intended to give the phrase force, in fact gives an impression of thoughtlessness and so makes it flabby.

Type and -type. The word **type** (in the sense of 'kind') is of course a noun; but the invention of the E-type Jaguar probably contributed to the popularity of its use, with an adjective or another noun, or both, to form an adjectival phrase, as in **Sorites type paradoxes, slippery slope type argument** and **Ingham type evasion**; occasionally the word **type**, in such constructions, will be preceded by a hyphen. This construction verges on slang; it is confusing to the reader, extremely ugly in itself, and quite unnecessary. Far preferable are **paradoxes of the Sorites type, argument** of the 'slippery slope' type and evasion of the type practised by Ingham. The noun style is less frequently, but just as objectionably, used in this way.

Vogue words. There are two reasons for avoiding a vogue word while the vogue lasts. First, any reader who has noticed the recent frequency of its occurrence will be irritated by it. Secondly, the usual result of its being used by many writers on every possible occasion is that its meaning becomes exceedingly vague. A good current example is the word **target**, used as a verb. In an article by four hands in the *Observer* (22 November 1992) on an aspect of Iraqgate there occurred the sentence **Lear Fan ... was targeted by Gerald Bull and TDG ... to build carbon fibre helmet cones**. The reader gathers that Bull and TDG wanted Lear Fan to build the cones; but whether they succeeded and, if so, by what means, is left wholly unclear.

Two principles sometimes cited are excessively rigorous:

(1) *And and But.* It is generally held to be bad to begin a sentence with a conjunction such as **and** or **but,** on the ground that it is the business of a conjunction to *conjoin* two clauses within a single sentence. Doing so incessantly, as news broadcasters do, only irritates; but the rule is not inviolable. Blake, after all, began a whole poem (within a poem) with **and**:

And did those feet in ancient time
Walk upon England's mountains green?

(2) *Ending a sentence with a preposition.* **What did you choose that book to be read to out of for?** is certainly to be deprecated; but

A fixed figure for the time of scorn
To point his slow unmoving finger at. (*Othello*)

is equally certainly to be applauded. The objection to ending a sentence with a preposition derives from the fact that in English we have *pre*positions (as against the *post*positions used in Japanese), and that they should therefore precede the noun or pronoun they govern. The problem is that there often is no such noun or pronoun; there is then no reason why you should not, with Shakespeare, place the preposition at the end of the sentence, if that is the natural place for it to go. Like any figure, this comes to grate if used too frequently, and can usually be easily avoided by recasting the sentence. When a preposition governs the relative pronoun introducing a relative clause, it is usually better to place it before that pronoun than at the end of the clause, even when the clause does not end the sentence; but this principle is far from exceptionless. Consider the relative clause **to which we have agreed not to add or take away** (R. Lane Fox, 1991); **which** here refers back to **contents**, and the clause does conclude the sentence. The writer obviously did not mean that we have agreed not to take away *to* the contents, but *from* them, so the clause needs emendation; but how should it be emended? **To which we have agreed not to add and from which we have agreed not to take away** is grammatically unobjectionable, but long-winded. **Not to add to, or take away from, which we have agreed** is intolerably clumsy. The only solution is to write **which we have agreed not to add to or take away from**.

Placing of prepositions. It follows from the preceding entry that a preposition need not always have a pronoun or noun-phrase to govern: neither in **He now faced the dangers he had been warned against** nor in **The dangers he had been warned against now threatened him** is there any need to rewrite **he had been warned against** as **against which he had been warned**. One should, however, avoid following a preposition by a pronoun or noun-phrase it might be wrongly taken, even if only momentarily, to govern. Thus a hasty reader of the sentence **He had promised those he had relied on the fruits of victory** might at first take **on** to govern **the fruits of victory**; better, therefore, to write **He had promised those on whom he had relied the fruits of victory** or **He had promised the fruits of victory to those he had relied on**. A worse ungainliness results from taking the noun-phrase to be understood, with the consequence that one preposition follows another: a recent article on unemployment by Simon Jenkins (*Times*, 17 February 1993) was marred by the sentence **to be jobless in London must be a wholly different concept from in Liverpool or Sunderland**. Since a preposition cannot govern an infinitive in English, gerunds need to be used instead: **being jobless in London must be a wholly diferent concept from being jobless in Liverpool or Sunderland** or **being jobless must be a wholly different concept in London and in Liverpool or Sunderland**. (The sentence is also marred by the inaccurate use of the word **concept**: the *concept* of unemployment – what it means to say that someone is unemployed – is the same in London and in Liverpool: it is the experience or the situation of the unemployed that is different.) When a preposition is the last word of its clause or part of an infinitive such as **to copy from** or **to be copied from,** it may stand without a noun-phrase or pronoun to govern; in all other cases, it *should* be followed by one.

Stock examples. Some unknown philosopher, about forty years ago, wanting an example of an word with two distinct meanings that could be used to frame an ambiguous sentence, fastened on the word **bank.** Since then, every philosopher, professional or student, has used the very same example, which must have occurred in many thousands of books, articles, theses and answers to examination questions. The language is full of words with multiple meanings – **fair** and **race** to cite two – that can be used to construct ambiguous sentences quite as plausible as **I am going to the bank**; yet no one has expended a moment's thought on devising a new example. It is overpoweringly *boring* to keep encountering examples met with hundreds of times before; and it strongly suggests paucity of imagination on the writer's part.

Scaffolding. In writing an essay, article or chapter, you should always be vividly conscious of the structure you mean it to have, and keep asking yourself whether that is the best structure for it. That structure should, however, be apparent from what you write: you should not waste time and bore the reader by *telling* him what the structure is; he should be able to see that for himself, and, if he cannot, you have written badly. The completed piece of writing should have no scaffolding around it. Thus, do not begin a paragraph with:

We have now discussed the apparent causes of the occurrence. It is impossible to determine whether these were in fact the real causes without knowing whether Saint-Just was aware of Robespierre's intentions. Hence, before we go on to enquire into the real causes, we must at this point in our discussion insert a brief digression directed towards finding the answer to this preliminary question.

Before he gets on to the substance of what you have to say, the reader will have had to plough through three whole dead sentences that tell him nothing about the subject-matter, but only about your arrangement of your discussion of it; and, by the time he has done so, he may well have forgotten what the question was on which you were meaning to focus his attention. The first sentence in the foregoing piece of scaffolding is entirely redundant: if the reader does not know what you have been discussing, he cannot have been paying any attention at all. The reason for your turning aside to discuss what Saint-Just knew may not yet be apparent: if you write clearly, it will become apparent soon enough; so the second sentence is also redundant. As for the third sentence, you should not *tell* the reader that you are going to insert a digression: you should simply *insert* it. Likewise, you should not announce that you are going to answer a certain question: you should simply *ask* it. The whole of the above deadly piece of scaffolding should therefore be replaced by:

Did Saint-Just know of Robespierre's intentions?

Split infinitives. The **to** with the infinitive is not a preposition, as it is in **he objects to examining in two schools**, but an integral part of the infinitive, which does not occur without it save after an auxiliary like **can** or **might**, in common but exceptional constructions like **she let him go** and after the conjunctions **and** and **or**, as in **to go and see**; in the last of these cases, the insertion of one or more words between the conjunction and the verb, for example in the phrase **to go and quickly find**, is a tacit split infinitive. Milton used a tacit split infinitive in his lines:

**To tend the homely, slighted shepherd's trade,
And strictly meditate the thankless Muse?** (*Lycidas*)

It is because **to** is integral to the infinitive that we speak of **the verb 'to leave'** and the like. For this reason, split infinitives are almost always ugly. Their defenders invariably remark that they are not ungrammatical, which is doubtless true; but the line between the strictly ungrammatical and the inelegant or unnatural is very thin. No native English speaker would ever say **He planted firmly his feet upon the ground** instead of **He planted his feet firmly upon the ground** or **He firmly planted his feet upon the ground**, and any Teach-yourself-English book would tell its readers that the position between a transitive verb and its object is not an acceptable one for an adverb in English; but to call the first of these sentences 'ungrammatical' would probably be to stretch that term somewhat. It is simply contrary to the spirit of the language to employ such a word order; and it is likewise contrary to the spirit of the language to divide the root verb from its accompanying **to**; English is after all a member of the Germanic family, and in German **zu** clings so tenaciously to the parent verb as to intervene between the root and the prefix, as in **unter-zunehmen,** of which the English equivalent would be **undertotake** (for **to undertake**). (An advertisement for a language school displayed in a New York bus asked **Wünschen Sie zu Englisch lernen?** [i.e. **Do you wish to English learn?**], and would certainly have found no takers.) It is true that the very recent popularity of the split infinitive has greatly weakened the impression of unnaturalness which the construction makes on those native speakers who read very little of anything written more than twenty years ago. (Fanny Burney is the only one of our classic authors to split her infinitives more than very occasionally; she does it as often in a three-volume novel as an average candidate in an Oxford Finals examination might in answers to a single paper.) Evidence that the practice nevertheless *is* unnatural to the language will be given below.

We have not yet reached a point at which an unsplit infinitive sounds offensive to anybody, whereas split infinitives still sound offensive to many. It is therefore sensible, if you want your writing to be found acceptable, to avoid them altogether; only a writer as good as Milton should even take the risk of using *tacit* split infinitives. Three categories of split infinitive must be avoided at all costs:

(1) the negative split, such as **to not admit** and **to no longer rely.** (Examples by Susan Sontag, 1992, are **It was pleasurable to not always know more** and **I have to not botch the telling.**) This has become increasingly common; unless resisted, it is only a question of time before we hear an actor declaim **To be or to not be.** It is nevertheless hideous, and *can* definitely be termed 'ungrammatical': it is as much a rule of English grammar that the negative particle should precede the **to** as it is a rule of French grammar that, with the infinitive, **ne pas** precedes the verb but follows the preposition. Particularly to be avoided is the construction used in **to no more than go through the motions: to do no more than go through the motions** is needed.

(2) the booby-trapped split. This consists of splitting the infinitive with a word that can be a verb, as in **to please go, to better understand, to further investigate.** The phrase **to even further discuss** contains a double booby-trap. The booby-trap always jolts the reader as he realises that what he had taken to be a verb is in fact an adverb; but connoisseurs of readers' discomfort have a further trick up their sleeves. In an article some years ago in the *Scientific American,* the author repeatedly used phrases like **to better understand** until he had conditioned the reader to expect a verb to follow **to better;** he then wrote a sentence containing a

phrase like **to better research opportunities,** with **better,** this time, as the verb.

(3) the multiple split. This is the insertion of more than one word between **to** and the infinitive, as in **to quite precisely determine.** The most outrageous example of the multiple split I have encountered is due to an American writer, Robert Wang:

> ... **inspired three of the members to (while not abrogating their oaths of membership) widely disseminate ...**

The construction **to more than,** as in **to more than complain,** is even more objectionable than **to no more than.** No one would say **He more than looked: he stared,** rather than **He did more than look: he stared;** to do so would be a *grammatical* mistake, since **more than** cannot govern a finite verb, but only an infinitive without **to.** In the same way, it is mandatory to say **He decided to do more than complain** instead of **He decided to more than complain.**

Those who have long been accustomed to split their infinitives but have been persuaded to abandon the practice frequently experience difficulty in knowing where to place the adverb or adverbial phrase. Often they simply place it in front of the **to,** producing such expressions as **Peter resolved quietly to creep along the corridor** and **Helen endeavoured very exactly to copy the drawing.** These look awkward, and are in some degree ambiguous: the first suggests that Peter took the resolution in a quiet, rather than noisy, manner, and the second that it was Helen's *endeavour* that was exact. To think where to put the adverb, it suffices to think where it would go when it qualified a finite form of the verb. You would in these examples most naturally put it after the verb and after the object, if any, saying **Peter crept quietly along the corridor** and **Helen copied the drawing very exactly,** and you should therefore likewise say **Peter resolved to creep quietly along the corridor** and **Helen endeavoured to copy the drawing very exactly.** In other cases, the natural place for the adverb would be *before* the verb; you should then put it before the **to.** If you are meaning to say what someone probably did (rather than to which of various possible correspondents she was writing), you will say **She probably wrote to George,** rather than **She wrote probably to George;** hence (on the same assumption) **I expected her to probably write to George** should be converted into **I expected her probably to write to George.** In **Are we courageously to resist, or faint-heartedly to surrender?** the adverbs come before the **to** because we should say

These men courageously resisted, but those faint-heartedly surrendered. The adverbs precede the verb because it is not being said that the former group resisted in a courageous rather than a timorous manner, or that the latter surrendered in a faint-hearted rather than a resolute fashion, but that it was courageous of the former to resist, faint-hearted of the latter to surrender. Sometimes two adverbs will need to be placed differently; for instance, **I expected her to probably first write to George** may need to be transformed into **I expected her probably to write first to George**.

This last example provides an excellent illustration of the ambiguities sometimes created by split infinitives. **I expected her first to write to George** means that I expected her to write to George before doing anything else, whereas **I expected her to write first to George** means that I expected her to write to George before she wrote to anyone else; **I expected her to first write to George** is ambiguous between the two. The reason is that the placing of the adverb with respect to the infinitive makes the same distinction of meaning as does its placing with respect to a finite verb, the distinction between **She first wrote to George** and **She wrote first to George**; but its placing between the **to** and the verb root, being intrinsically unnatural, corresponds to neither and thereby obliterates the distinction. Ambiguities of this type provide the strongest evidence that to split infinitives is to violate the spirit of the language. Another example is **He proceeded to boldly answer his accusers**. **He answered his accusers boldly** means that he answered them in a bold fashion; **He boldly answered his accusers** implies that it was bold of him to answer them at all. **He proceeded to answer his accusers boldly** gives the former sense, and **He boldly proceeded to answer his accusers** the latter; **He proceeded to boldly answer his accusers** is ambiguous between the two, since it was not until recently something that a native English speaker would normally say. Those who make a practice of splitting infinitives weaken their own sensitivity to such distinctions, and therewith their feeling for the language. Very often, a placing of the adverb anywhere but after **to** will come to sound unnatural to their ears: where else could it be put in **I did not dare to actually speak to him**, since **I did not actually dare to speak to him** has a subtly different meaning? The meaning they intend would be achieved, for someone who continues to resist the split infinitive, by **I did not dare actually to speak to him**; but they can no longer hear such a sentence as anything but awkward. If they are resolute, however, and revert to the traditional word-order, it will soon come to seem natural once more.

An argument sometimes adduced against the objection to split infinitives is that it is based on a false analogy with Latin; since the Latin infinitive is a single word, the English one had to be treated as one, too. If this had been the motive, there would have been a similar objection to inserting an adverb after the auxiliary in English tensed verbs like **will go, has gone**, etc., since these are also single words in Latin; in fact, no one has ever raised any objection to this.

4. Punctuation

Punctuation is a feeble substitute for the devices of intonation and phrasing (in the musical sense) that are used in speech to dispel the ambiguity sentences and phrases would often otherwise have. Written sentences, being in general more complex, stand in more frequent danger of ambiguity; and a writer cannot correct a reader's misunderstanding, as a speaker can correct a hearer's. Writers should therefore use every means that language affords them for avoiding equivocal phraseology; besides adherence to syntactic rules, the chief of these is punctuation.

Yet punctuation is nowadays carelessly employed: the hyphen has virtually disappeared, apostrophes are omitted when needed and inserted when not wanted, commas are used in place of semi-colons, quotation marks are left out. This is a very foolish habit: since a writer's first aim should be to be understood, it makes no sense to spurn an aid to achieving it.

HYPHENS

The chief function of the hyphen is to make structure apparent. It is sometimes essential to avoid actual ambiguity, as in the phrase **staying on rates** cited under 3(c), or in **as seen in the cleaner fish** from the *Guardian* article by Pamela Wells referred to under 2(g); since, in the context, the fish in question were not those cleanlier than others, but those that cleansed others, **cleaner-fish** would have averted misunderstanding. More frequently, the lack of a simple hyphen will lead a reader to misconstrue only the beginning of the sentence, later finding that he has to go back and read it again from the start.

An amusing consequence of the frequent failure to use a hyphen in the stock phrase **with a fine-tooth comb** is the tendency of many writers to insert it in the wrong place, writing **with a fine tooth-comb**; presumably a tooth-comb accompanies a toothbrush.

When a noun is used as part of an adjectival phrase, it normally requires a hyphen to alert the reader to the fact that it does not have its usual role as a noun. This applies both when the noun is the first, and when it is the second, of two words forming the adjectival phrase. When it is the second of two words forming a common phrase, the first of the two being an adjective or participle, and the phrase is being used as a noun-phrase, no hyphen is required, because the adjective or participle leads the reader to expect, correctly, that a noun is coming. There is therefore no need for a hyphen in common phrases like **fishing boat, bathing dress, stepping stone** and **playing card**, in contexts like **stepping stones to higher things** and **a pack of playing cards**.

When such phrases are used adjectivally, however, as in **playing-card factory, sailing-boat design**, and the like, a hyphen is needed, to prevent the slight jolt the reader may otherwise have when he finds a second noun following the first. In recent academic writing, and in philosophy at least as much as in any other subject, a vogue has arisen for compound adjectival phrases of which the *first* of two words is the noun, like **structure-preserving, theory-laden, theory-dependent** and many others, which, of course, have *only* an adjectival use, unlike phrases of the **fishing boat** type. These even more require a hyphen, because, without one, the reader is extremely likely to mistake the syntax; he may even at first think that the participle or adjective qualifies the noun preceding it, only to have to go back to read the sentence again: if you write **is embedded in a structure independent way**, he will be expecting **of** when he reaches **independent**, will receive a jolt when he does not get it, and will have to go back and read the clause again from the beginning. Courtesy to the reader is not a sign of weakness; the lack of it is a symptom of incompetent writing.

The use of these barbarous compounds is not wholly avoidable, but it should be avoided when possible, e.g. by the substitution of **All reports of observation depend on theory** for **All observation reports are theory-dependent**, of **independently of context** for **in a context-independent manner** and of **preserves structure** for **is structure-preserving**. The attempt to turn academic English into Chinese may succeed; if it does, it will no longer be English, but a descendant of it.

APOSTROPHES

The principal use of the apostrophe is to indicate an omitted letter or sequence of letters, as in **isn't, doesn't, wouldn't** and the like, where the apostrophe indicates the omitted letter o. An old-fashioned way of writing the colloquial **shan't** was therefore **sha'n't**, with the first apostrophe indicating the missing double **l**; but this would nowadays look hopelessly pedantic.

In the same way, when the phrase **it is** is abbreviated by leaving out the **i** of **is**, an apostrophe must be inserted, to form **it's**; one should never write **Oh no its not** (A. Anthony, *Guardian*, 14 December 1991). The genitive or possessive form of a singular noun should also always be written with an apostrophe, as in **Russell's theory** or **the dog's bone**. This apostrophe is supposed originally to have indicated an abbreviation for **Russell his theory** or **the dog his bone**, but these phrases are far too archaic to provide a justification for it today. It has been retained because it is useful as distinguishing between the genitive and the plural, for instance between **Russell's** in **Russell's theory** and **Russells** in **The Russells have always been obstinate**. In the genitive of a plural noun, the apostrophe follows the **s**, as in **the dogs' bowls**.

The same rule used to be observed (in both pronunciation and spelling) for the genitive of a proper name ending in **s**, as in **Jones' hat**; but the present convention is to add an **'s** in the same way as to any other name, and to pronounce the result accordingly: thus **Jones's hat**.

Possessive pronouns, on the other hand, have never had an apostrophe. This is because they have special forms of their own, such as **my**, not all ending in **s**, and because the possessive form **his** is obviously not an abbreviation for **he his**. In particular, the possessive form of **it** is **its**, *without* an apostrophe: you write **its origin**, *not* **it's origin**. To insert the apostrophe suggests confusion of mind; it also obliterates the useful distinction between the possessive **its** and the abbreviation **it's** of **it is**.

No possessive personal pronoun carries an apostrophe: neither those that function like adjectives (**my, your, his, her, its, our, their** and **thy**), nor those that function like nouns (**mine, yours, his, hers, its, ours, theirs** and **thine**). Nor does **whose**, the possessive form of the relative pronouns **who** and **which**; **who's** can only be an abbreviation of **who is**. Even an eight-year-old ought to be ashamed of the use, conversely, of **whose** in place of **who's**, as in **And if so, whose to blame?** (*Guardian* sub-headline, 14 December 1991), a confusion between **whose fault is it?** and **who's to blame?**

COLONS AND SEMI-COLONS

A colon is used before a list, or before a specification of any other kind; in **He did not merely weaken the basis of the Papal claim: he annihi-**

lated it and **He trounced his enemies: those who had so savagely criticised his first book,** the part of each sentence after the colon counts, for this purpose, as a specification. If the items of a list following a colon are too long to be separated by mere commas, they should be separated by semi-colons. Except in this case, a sentence will rarely tolerate more than one semi-colon or more than one colon within it, though it can more easily accommodate one colon and one semi-colon. As is apparent from the second example above, a colon does not demand a complete clause after it; even when a complete clause follows, this does *not* normally begin with a capital letter. A semi-colon does demand to be followed by a complete clause, save when separating the items of a list. Semi-colons are used when a long sentence demands more of a pause than a comma provides, but the second half is too closely connected to the first to warrant a full stop.

THE QUESTION MARK

Some languages demand an exclamation mark after an imperative. English does not; but it does demand a question mark after a question. Its omission, as in

So why do we go along.

(A. Anthony, *Guardian*, 14 December 1991), merely displays a foolish contempt for the use of punctuation altogether. It is easy to forget the question mark after a request (**Could you please tell me whether ...**) or a rhetorical question (**Would anyone conclude from that ...**); but it should not be forgotten.

QUOTATION MARKS

Unless (as here) some other device is being employed, a word or expression that is being referred to rather than used should always be enclosed in quotation marks. It is irritating to read **She always avoided toilet, preferring almost any circumlocution,** when what is meant is that she avoid using the *word* "toilet"; the sentence should read **She always avoided "toilet",** ... Quoted expressions or speeches within quoted speeches should be signalised by alternating single and double quotation marks, to enable the reader to keep track thus: **"His reply", she went on,**

"could not have been bettered. 'My advice to you is,' he said, 'in the words of Sam Goldwyn, "Don't even ignore them" ' ".

As here, before words that interrupt the quotation (typically, **he said** and the like), the quotation marks are closed, and reopened after them. If a new paragraph occurs *within* the quotation, it begins with open quotation marks, repeated, although the preceding paragraph is not closed by quotation marks, thus:

> **"I will not detain you long," he began, "but I cannot let the occasion pass without saying a few words.**
>
> **"It seems only yesterday that I first met our guest of honour. He was no more than a youngster, then, but already ...".**

Quotation marks have two main uses, between which are some intermediate cases. The first is to cite the words uttered or written by some actual or imaginary individual, or to pick out a word, phrase or sentence *about* which something is to be said, as in **"Fast" may be an adjective or an abverb**. In this use, the quoted word or words are not being *used*, but only referred to. In the second use, the writer *is* using the word or phrase, but wishes to indicate that the use is in some way special or unusual; very often, he is copying the terminology of one or more others, from which he wants to distance himself. Quotation marks so used are slangily called 'sneer quotes'. We have, in English, two kinds of quotation marks, double and single; clarity is served by using them to differentiate the two uses, employing double ones for the first of the two, and single ones for the second; intermediate cases, such as **are called 'sneer quotes'**, may be treated as the writer prefers. It is not feasible to do the converse, since single quotation marks are naturally felt to be lighter than double ones. The practice now well-nigh universal among publishers, to use single quotation marks for actual quotations, therefore has the effect of making it impossible to mark the distinction typographically, which is a pity.

COMMAS, WITH RELATIVE CLAUSES AND OTHERWISE

Commas frequently come in pairs, to separate off some phrase or clause, somewhat as a pair of brackets does; the choice is thus often between two commas or none. An example of this occurs with relative clauses. Such a clause ought to be enclosed in commas when it does not serve to define the person or thing referred to, but merely adds supplementary information, as in **The invigilator, who had sat up all night marking papers, fell asleep during the examination**: the omission of the relative clause still leaves a sentence unambiguously conveying part of the information – **The invigilator fell asleep during the examination.**

When the relative clause is essential to determine the reference, however, no commas are needed: the deletion of the relative clause from **The dog to which he threw the bone obstructed him no further** would leave the reference indeterminate. When the relative clause is of this second kind, and the relative pronoun is its subject or its object, **that** is preferable to **which,** and often to **who: the hat that I bought yesterday** is usually better than **the hat which I bought yesterday.** This principle is not sacrosanct, however; for instance, if there are already two occurrences of **that** in the sentence, **which** should be preferred.

A parenthetical phrase should usually be inserted at a natural break; it is usually unobjectionable to put an adverbial phrase between an auxiliary verb like **has** or **is** and a participle, but not between a preposition and the noun-phrase it governs. A sentence like **they are related to, on the one hand, Goodman's irrealism and, on the other hand, Saussure's form of the doctrine of incommensurability** (H. Putnam) reads very jerkily. A definite improvement would be **they are related, on the one hand, to Goodman's irrealism and, on the other, to Saussure's form of the doctrine of incommensurability.** Even better would be either **they are related to Goodman's irrealism on the one hand and, on the other, to Saussure's form of the doctrine of incommensurability** or **they are related to Goodman's irrealism on the one hand, and to Saussure's form of the doctrine of incommensurability on the other.** (See *Parallel phrases* in Section 3 for the omission of the second occurrence of **hand.**)

A comma should not normally be used to separate two independent clauses not joined by any conjunction; unless a conjunction is inserted, at least a semi-colon is needed. Likewise, two or more parallel words or phrases should be connected by a conjunction. This does not apply to adjectives preceding the same noun, nor to noun-phrases with the same reference (in apposition): **her long silky hair; to Scotland, my native land.** When there are three or more words, phrases or clauses joined by a single occurrence of **and** or **or** before the last of them, a comma should follow all but the last two, but should not precede the conjunction, thus: **Sam, Dick, Tom or Harry.** (Oxford University Press is very proud of putting a comma before the conjunction – after **Tom,** in the example –

calling it 'the Oxford comma'; but no comma is needed to separate a word or phrase from the conjunction that links it to another.)

It would be hard to give rules dissolving all perplexity about whether or not to use commas to separate adjectives qualifying the same noun. Some adjectives, like **good, average** and **leading**, are relative to a whole class; commas must then be distributed appropriately. For instance, **the principal female instructor** refers to the female instructor of more importance than the other female instructors, whereas **the principal, female, instructor** refers to the instructor of more importance than the other instructors, adding the information that she is female; the fact that she is the *principal instructor* accounts for the second comma. By inverting the order of the adjectives to obtain **the female principal instructor**, we avoid the need for commas; but this cannot be done to **the second, main, verb of the sentence**. This of course refers to the second verb occurring in the sentence, pointing out parenthetically that it is the main verb; without the commas, it would refer to the second of the main verbs (if there could be such a thing). An extension of this principle is that an adjective regarded as helping to specify what is being talked about, rather than merely supplying an additional description of it, stands immediately in front of the noun, while a preceding adjective is not followed by a comma. Thus there is no comma in **her beautiful tame leopard**; the phrase is more naturally thought of as referring to a tame leopard than merely to a leopard. Adjectives felt to serve a parallel descriptive purpose are separated by a comma, as in **a hairy, smelly dog**; there is no need for a comma between **smelly** and **dog**, because **hairy** is not relative to the class of dogs as **principal** was relative to the class of instructors or **second** to the class of verbs.

A word such as **However** or **Nevertheless**, or a phrase like **Despite this**, should always be followed by a comma when it begins a sentence. This is important for averting misunderstanding when **However** is followed by an adjective or adverb. In

However much time was wasted in reminiscence, they ended by resolving their disagreement.

the clause up to the comma is a subordinate one with a concessive force, whereas

However, much time was wasted in reminiscence.

is a complete sentence. If, in the latter, the comma is omitted, the reader will be expecting a main clause when he reaches the end of the sentence, and will then realise that he had been misled. **Therefore**, if placed at the head of the sentence, should be followed by a comma; but it is normally better style to place it later in the sentence, usually without commas, but sometimes enclosed between two. Thus **There is therefore no need** ... is in most cases to be preferred to **Therefore, there is no need** ... .

BRACKETS AND FULL STOPS

If an entire sentence is enclosed in brackets, the full stop precedes the closing bracket; but if the phrase in brackets is only part of the sentence which it concludes, the full stop comes after the bracket. Thus it is wrong to write:

He admitted the theft (but not the forgery.)

It should be:

He admitted the theft (but not the forgery).

Conversely, one should write:

(He admitted the theft, but not the forgery.)

rather than:

(He admitted the theft, but not the forgery).

5. Vocabulary

Affect and effect. The verb **to effect** means 'to bring about' or 'to accomplish', while **to affect** means 'to have some effect on'.

Alternative(ly) and alternate(ly). **Alternatively** means 'another possibility is that'; **alternately** means 'first one, then the other, then the one again, and so on': similarly for the adjectives. The two ought never to be confused, though they persistently are. Since the noun **alternative** has already the sense of 'another possibility', **there is another alternative** is a pleonasm; one should say merely **there is an alternative**. (Mrs Thatcher's slogan was "There Is No Alternative", not "There Is No *Other* Alternative".)

An allied mistake is to write **there is only one alternative** when you mean that there is only one possible course of action, plausible hypothesis or the like, i.e. that there is *no* alternative. Much as with the word **copy** (which permits the original to be referred to as **the top copy**), it is allowable to speak of the possibility first mentioned as **the first alternative**, and the alternative subsequently mentioned as **the second alternative**. Strictly speaking, there cannot be a third. To insist on this is somewhat pedantic, however: Gladstone spoke of four alternatives and J. S. Mill of three.

Argumentum ad hominem. The phrase **argumentum ad hominem**, or **ad hominem argument**, refers to an argument against a proposition held by a particular individual, whose force depends on particular facts about that individual, especially concerning other beliefs that he holds; it may, for example, seek to demonstrate an inconsistency between the proposition and those other beliefs.

It is a mistake to replace **ad hominem** by **ad feminam** when the individual concerned is a woman, because the Latin word **homo** (of which **hominem** is the accusative) means 'human being' irrespective of sex, as do the Greek word **anthropos** and the German word **Mensch**; all three languages have separate words for 'man' in the sense of 'adult human male' (**vir, aner** and **Mann** respectively).

-ation, -ate. Abstract nouns ending in **-ation**, such as **creation**, are often formed from verbs ending in **-ate**; but a great many, like **causation**, are not. A mistake frequently made by those whose mother-tongue is not English is to form the verb incorrectly from the abstract noun by the reverse process – known as back-formation – producing such absurdities as **to annexate**. The only mistake of this kind commonly made by native English speakers is to use the verb **to administrate**, created by back-formation from **administration**; the correct form is **to administer**. The deplorable word **commentate** is not even a back-formation, since the noun is **commentary** and not **commentation**.

Beg the question. The phrase **to beg the question** does *not* mean the same as **to ask the question** or **to raise the question**. It means 'to offer an argument for some conclusion which depends, for its validity, upon assuming the truth of that very conclusion'; this fallacy is also known as a **petitio principii**, but the homely **begging the question** is usually to be preferred. To use **to beg**, in this context, with the sense of **to ask** or **to raise** is to court misunderstanding, and to risk depriving the language of a useful phrase, with no compensating advantage.

Categorial, categorical. The adjective **categorical** means 'not hypothetical' or 'not conditional': to deny something *categorically* is to deny it without provisos or reservations. **Categorial**, a much rarer word, means 'relating to categories': in assigning two things to different categories, you make a *categorial* distinction between them.

Cohort. The word **cohort** denotes a Roman military unit. It has been purloined by sociologists to mean, quite inappropriately, a group defined by age, and is a vogue word with the indefinite sense of 'category' or 'class'. As so used, it is irritating because modish and imprecise. It can, of course, be used figuratively, but should be confined to contexts in which it carries the sense of a group banded together for defence or attack. Its use to mean 'colleague' is inexcusable.

Comprise. The Cabinet *comprises* the principal Ministers, or, equivalently, *consists of* them; it should *not* be said to **comprise of** them or to **be comprised of** them. The principal Ministers *compose* or *(together) constitute* the Cabinet; to say that they **comprise** it is to use that verb as having a sense inverse to its true meaning.

Construal. In the past twenty years, philosophers who write in English have made regular use of the word **construal**, as meaning 'way of construing' or 'interpretation'. The *Oxford English Dictionary*, however, does not recognise the existence of the word, giving the noun from **to construe** as **construction** (as in **to put a sinister construction on the facts**). The attitude taken to this will depend on temperament.

Critique. The word **critique** is a noun, principally used in translations of the titles of Kant's writings. It cannot properly be used as a verb; according to what the writer wishes to convey, it should be replaced by **criticise, evaluate, examine** or some similar word. A horrible example, garnished with a split infinitive, is **to lovingly understand and critique all aspects of life** (from an article about the purpose of education in *The Allen Review*, Michaelmas 1991).

Decimate. **To decimate** means 'to reduce *by* a tenth', not 'to reduce *to* a tenth', and derives from the Roman practice of lining men up and killing every tenth man; if it had been to *spare* every tenth man, what reason could there have been not to kill the lot?

Defuse and diffuse. The transitive verb **to defuse** means 'to remove the fuse from' an explosive device, thus rendering it harmless; it may be used metaphorically, with an object that is (metaphorically) explosive. The verb **to diffuse**, which can be transitive or intransitive, means 'to spread widely' or 'to soften' (as of light). The two verbs should not be confused.

Deprecate and *depreciate*. This is another pair of verbs liable to be confused. **To deprecate** is a transitive verb meaning 'to express disapproval of'. **To depreciate** may be used transitively or intransitively, and means 'to lessen in value' or, figuratively, 'to belittle'.

Disambiguate. Like the noun **construal**, the transitive verb **disambiguate**, meaning 'to render (something) unambiguous that would otherwise have been ambiguous', is not accorded recognition by the *Oxford English Dictionary*. Some people regard it as ugly, others as performing a useful function. The choice is the reader's.

Disinterested and uninterested. Probably all University students know the difference between these two words. To be *uninterested* in chemistry is not to find chemistry interesting. To be *disinterested* is to be impartial and uninfluenced by personal advantage in a judgement or decision. The practice is widespread of using **disinterested** to mean **uninterested**, and not using **uninterested** at all. If it prevails, a word will have been pointlessly lost to the language; it should therefore be resisted.

Dissociate. The opposite of **associate** is **dissociate**, not **disassociate**; there is no such word as **disassociate**.

Exact. **Exact** does not have the same grammar as **same**; it ought not to be used as a comparative followed by **as**, as it is in **Mark ... happened to arrive in Oman at the exact time as his mother** (A. Raphael, *Observer*, 15 December 1991). Either **at exactly the same time as his mother** or **at the exact time that his mother did** is needed.

Feedback. A mechanical system involves *feedback* if it monitors its own operation, and is acted upon in turn as a result (the output is fed back into the input). For instance, if the flight of an aeroplane diverges to the right from the intended path, the automatic pilot is made to deflect the plane to the left (and likewise in other cases): in this way the plane is kept very accurately on course. This is *negative feedback*, the effect of any divergence from the intended course of the operation being opposite in sense to that divergence. If its sense were the same, for example if divergence to the right caused further deflection to the right, there would be *positive feedback*: in most cases, this would be catastrophic.

The word **feedback** should be reserved for this precise technical meaning, and not misused to mean 'response' or 'comment'; such misuse, intended to display the scientific sophistication of the writer, in fact advertises his ignorance. A characteristic actual example is **a pilot recently concluded has, on balance, had very positive feedback (pilot** is here used to mean 'pilot scheme').

Flout and flaunt. **To flout** has the basic meaning 'to mock', but is now almost exclusively applied to the deliberate violation of a rule, principle, agreement or convention, usually with the implication that the violation is contemptuous. The verb **to flaunt** may be used transitively or intransitively, and means 'to show off by way of ostentatious display'. These verbs should not be confused, but often are, as in **Tudjman and Milosevic ... committed themselves solemnly to accords and agreements whose provisions they would openly flaunt the following day** (M. Glenny, 1992).

Imply and infer. Only a person can **infer**; one statement can **imply** another, which the speaker also **implied** by making the first statement. To **infer** something is to draw a conclusion; to say something from which that conclusion follows or which the speaker means his hearers to take as following is to **imply** the conclusion, *not* to **infer** it. Thus **The Chancellor inferred that taxes would have to be raised** means that he drew that conclusion; to express that he said something from which the conclusion could be drawn, **imply** needs to be used instead.

Infringe. **Infringe** is a transitive verb; it does not need, and should not have, **on** appended to it.

Key. The word **key**, which is of course a noun, is commonly used adjectivally in well-known phrases like **the key move**. It nevertheless retains its quality as a noun, and should not, therefore, be used as an adjective when it does not immediately precede a noun, as in the statement **Taxation is key** made by a Government minister during the last general election campaign.

Lean. As a noun or adjective, **lean** is opposed to **fat**, as in

**Let me have men about me that are fat,
Sleek-headed men and such as sleep o' nights.
Yon Cassius has a lean and hungry look.** (*Julius Caesar*),

or the nursery rhyme:

**Jack Sprat would eat no fat,
His wife would eat no lean.**

The verb **to lean** means 'to diverge from the vertical', literally or metaphorically, as in **the leaning tower of Pisa**. The *noun* **lean** cannot be used in a cognate sense, however; **slant** (or **tilt**) should be used instead.

Lie and lay. For this important pair, see 2(f).

Lose and loose. The verb **to lose** (with voiced **s**) means 'to mislay', the verb **to loose** (with unvoiced **s**) 'to set free' or 'to discharge'. It is a serious piece of illiteracy to confuse them.

Meld. The verb **to meld** has recently come to be used as meaning 'to combine' or (in a metaphorical sense) 'to fuse', presumably from an impression that it is a portmanteau of **merge** and **weld**. It is in fact derived from German **melden** = 'to announce', and means to declare a scoring combination of cards (e.g. three Kings) in a game such as rummy.

Masterful and masterly. **Masterful**, which means 'dominating', is often used erroneously for **masterly** in the sense of 'worthy of the master of a skill'.

Militate and mitigate. These two verbs should likewise not be confused. **To militate against** something is to work against it, particularly as evidence against its truth; **to mitigate** is to moderate or alleviate (for instance, by reducing the seriousness of an offence).

Momentarily. **Momentarily** means 'for a moment', not 'in a moment'; but do not be alarmed if you hear an American airline pilot say **We are about to momentarily take off,** as they frequently do.

Overly. This ugly adverb, common in America, is redundant: **too** or **excessively** should be used instead.

Perspicuous, perspicacious, percipient. Only a person can be said to be **perspicacious** or **percipient**, namely capable of acute discernment; things such as distinctions and modes of expression are said to be **perspicuous**, that is, (in a metaphorical sense) plain to view.

Prefer and preference. The right construction is **she prefers fish to meat**, not **she prefers fish rather than meat**. It is quite unidiomatic to replace the preposition **to** simply by **than**; **rather than** should be used only when the verb **prefer** is followed by an infinitive, as in **He prefers to write rather than (to) telephone** and **Do you prefer to ride a bicycle rather than a horse?** In such contexts, it is more elegant to avoid either the infinitive or the verb **to prefer**, for instance by **He prefers writing to telephoning** or **Would you rather ride a bicycle than a horse?** The noun

preference takes a different construction, as in **her preference for fish over meat**. (For **rather**, see 2(b), *Comparison of adjectives*.)

Preventive. As an adjective, the form is **preventive**, *not* **preventative**. Use may claim to have sanctioned the longer form as a noun, but it is still unnecessary; we do not, after all, speak of **preventation**.

Prominent and predominant. **Prominent** means 'standing out so as to be highly noticeable'. **Predominant** means 'prevailing', and may be applied to that which has more influence, is more widely used or practised, or enjoys greatest popularity. Note the differently spelled terminations.

Refute and deny. To **deny** something is to say that it is not so: to **refute** it is to *prove* that it is not so. You should not say that someone **refuted** a proposition unless you yourself accept that he demonstrated it to be false; otherwise he merely **denied** it.

Retraction and retractation. The transitive verb **to retract** is used in two senses, a literal and a figurative one. In its literal sense, it means 'to draw (something) back', as when a cat retracts or sheathes its claws; in the figurative sense, it means 'to take back' an assertion or the like. Two different abstract nouns correspond to these two senses of the verb: **retraction** to the literal sense, and **retractation** to the figurative one. It is therefore wrong to use **retraction** to mean the act of withdrawing an assertion or claim.

Specious. The adjective **specious**, commonly applied to arguments, but also to stories, claims, etc., has for many years suffered from ambiguity. Its original meaning is 'plausible', without commitment to the soundness of the argument or the truth of the claim. Since it is naturally applied to arguments that appear convincing, but prove to be unsound, or to claims that appear just, but are in fact false, it is often used with almost the opposite meaning. Contrast **His reasoning is specious and he has more or less succeeded in soothing my tremors** (P. G. Wodehouse, speaking in the person of Bertie Wooster, 1971) with **For decades the Vatican has deployed a series of arguments, each more specious that the previous one** (C. Richards, *Independent*, 31 July 1992; **that** is obviously a misprint for **than**). Bertie Wooster (who often forgets words, but never misuses them) means that Jeeves's reasoning is convincing;

Richards means that each of the Vatican's arguments is *less* convincing than the previous one. In view of the ambiguity, it is best to avoid using **specious**; it should *not* be used to mean 'fallacious' or 'obviously false'.

Tantamount, paramount. **Tantamount** (which cannot precede a noun) means 'in effect equivalent'; **paramount** means 'supreme'. They should not be confused, as they are in **Going to the Earth Summit without signing the treaty on biodiversity is paramount to sitting in a car without putting the keys in the ignition** (leader in *Catholic Herald*, 5 June 1992). Some African rulers bear the title **Paramount Chief**; none is called **Tantamount Chief**.

Transpire. The verb **to transpire** does *not* mean 'to occur'. In its figurative sense, in which it is most often used, it means 'to come to light' (in the figurative sense of *this* expression).

Verbs from nouns. A habit has developed among commercial organisations in recent years of converting nouns into verbs, regardless of the established existence of those verbs in totally different senses. My first introduction to this practice was a notice in an American airport saying **This door is alarmed**. I took this to be a comic mistake; later examples have shown it to be a deliberate attempt to alter the language for the convenience of the company at the cost of impoverishing everyone else's vocabulary. The same notice, **This door is alarmed**, is to be seen on a door in Debenham's store in Oxford, and I have seen the even more ridiculous **This clock is alarmed** (*not* referring to an alarm clock) in a country house open (for a price) to the public. A similar example I recently heard was an announcement on an aeroplane, after landing, **You will be coached to the terminal building**. It is unnecessary here to explain that **to alarm** does not mean 'to fit with an alarm', nor **to coach** 'to take by coach'; it may be worth advising readers neither to imitate nor to countenance such arrogant vandalism.

6. Spelling

Spelling mistakes, though less heinous than grammatical errors, are even more common in University examination scripts. They often occur in the 'quality' Press, too; sentences like **During the winter of 1963-4, Labour lead by 8 to 12 points** (P. Kellner, *Independent*, 10 January 1992) cause momentary confusion, but have long ceased to cause surprise. Only the most frequent misspellings have been noted here, though many others are common in examination papers; but to warn against them all would require copying out most of the dictionary. The way to improve faulty spelling is to cultivate the habit of noting the spellings of words as one reads, making sure that much of what one reads was published more than twenty years ago and in Britain.

Although erratic, English spelling is governed by certain principles, almost all of them admitting plentiful exceptions. It is well to master these: someone who follows them blindly will be right far more often than he is wrong. Here are some of them:

(1) Except in some foreign words like **Iraq** and **Iraqi, q** always has **u** after it.

(2) The letters **c** and **g** have a hard sound before **a, o** and **u**, but a soft one before **e** and **i**. Compare **cork** and **cent, good** and **gin**. A **u** is sometimes added after **g** to make it hard, as in **guest** and **vague**.

(3) Short vowels are very seldom directly followed by **k**: contrast **break** and **sick**. Words ending in -c, like **panic** and **comic**, seldom have the stress on the last syllable. In monosyllables and words with the stress on the last syllable, -ck is usually used instead, as in **kick, back** and **attack**. The same applies to a stressed syllable followed by a consonant. Thus **particular** and **particle** have no **k**, the first because the **c** is followed by the vowel **u**, the second because the **i** is not stressed; but **fickle** fulfils both conditions, and hence has a **k**.

(4) The rule '**i** before **e** except after **c**' used to be drilled into children: compare **piece** and **perceive**. The rule is meant to apply to words in which the **i/e** combination is pronounced 'ee'; it does not hold for those like **reign** and **sovereign**.

Grammar & Style

(5) A vowel followed by a single consonant followed in turn by another vowel is usually long, even when the second vowel is the mute **e** in which so many English words end. Thus **pure**, **core**, **cake**, etc.; also **rodent**, **final** and so on. If the vowel is short, the consonant is probably doubled, as in **hammer**, **horrid** and **flannel**. There are numerous exceptions, however: the **o** in **probable** is one, and the **a** in **animal** another.

(6) Before **a**, **o** and **u**, the letter **c**, when doubled, has a -k- sound, as in **occur**. Before **e** and **i**, **cc** has the pronunciation -ks-, as in **succeed** and **accident**; an exception is the word **soccer** (at one time spelled **socker**). The letters **j**, **k**, **q**, **w**, **x** and **y** are never doubled, and **h** appears twice successively only in such compounds as **withhold**.

(7) When single **s** has a vowel before and after it (even when the latter is mute), it is usually voiced, i.e. pronounced -z-, as in **feasible** and **tease**. If the sound is unvoiced, i.e. a genuine -s- sound, either double **s** or (before **e** or **i**) **c** is likely to be used, as in **possible** and **placid**. Note that the **a** in **placid** is yet another exception to principle (5).

Accede, intercede, precede, proceed and succeed. These five verbs are spelled as here indicated. Since in all five cases the second syllable is derived from the same Latin verb, the reason for the difference in spelling is not immediately apparent: it has to do with the fact that the last two verbs have been in the language for longer than the first three.

Accommodate, accommodation. These words are often misspelled: they have two **c**'s and two **m**'s.

-ance and -ence. In British orthography, nouns ending thus are spelled with a **c** and *not* an **s**: **absence**, **attendance**, **dance**, **defence**, **licence**, **pretence**, **tolerance**.

Argument. The verb is spelled **argue**, but the noun **argument** (and not **arguement**).

Commit and omit. The verb **to commit** and its derivatives have two **m**'s; the verb **to omit** and its derivatives have only one.

Comparison and comparative. The noun is spelled **comparison**, but the adjective is spelled **comparative**.

Develop and envelop. The noun **envelope** is spelled with an **e** at the end, but the verb **to envelop** (like the word **potato**) without one. A recent habit is to spell **to develop** with a final **e**, as **develope**, but this is wrong. It may be due to the influence of **envelope** or a back-formation from the past tense **developed**, as **potatoe** is a back-formation from **potatoes**.

Disastrous. The noun is **disaster**, but the adjective is spelled **disastrous**, *not* **disasterous**; this common incorrect spelling is formed by false analogy with **murderous** and **thunderous**.

Disc. The word is spelled with a **c** in English; **disk** is an American spelling, like **skeptic** in place of **sceptic**.

Doubled consonant. Why should we write **referring** and **referred**, but **proffering** and **proffered**, **bestirring** and **bestirred**, but **desiring** and **desired**, **fretting** and **fretted**, but **deserting** and **deserted**? For once there is a simple rule. The final consonant is doubled when, in the simple (infinitive) form of the verb, it is immediately preceded by a short vowel and the stress is on the last syllable, otherwise not. Thus in **refer** the second syllable is stressed, in **proffer** the first, while, although in both **bestir** and **desire** the stress is on the second syllable, in **bestir** the **i** is short, whereas in **desire** it is long; and the **t** of **fret** is of course preceded by a vowel, while that of **desert** is preceded by the consonant **r**. Note particularly **focusing** and **focused** (with the stress on the first syllable). There are two (regular) exceptions to this rule. (1) The letter **l** is almost always doubled after a short vowel, even if it is not stressed: e.g. **labelling/labelled**, **levelling/levelled**, but **concealing/concealed**. The exception is the final **l** of **parallel**; **(un)paralleled** is spelled with only one **l** before **-ed**. (2) The letter **x** is never doubled: e.g. **fixing/fixed**, **relaxing/relaxed**.

Ecstasy. This word is so spelled, and not as **ecstacy**, because it comes from the Greek **stasis** and means 'standing outside oneself'.

Ensure and insure. To **ensure** something is to make certain that it is so or that it occurs. To **insure** something is to pay money to an insurance company, which will recompense you if it is lost, damaged or stolen.

For- and fore-. For those who know German, the prefix **for-** corresponds to German **ver-**, and the prefix **fore-** to German **vor-**. They have distinct meanings: **fore-** indicates precedence, temporal or otherwise, while **for-** has a privative sense. Thus you **forgo** something when you do without it, whereas the **foregoing** section is the one before this, and you cannot **forbear** to say (or refrain from saying) a word in praise of your **forebears** (or ancestors). Other examples are **forswear, forbid, forfeit, forfend, forget, forgive, forgo** and **forsake**, as contrasted with **foresee, forecast, foreboding, forefather, forenamed, foresight** and **foreshore**.

Fraternal twins. Two words pronounced so as to rhyme, but spelled differently, may be called 'fraternal twins': note in particular the pairs **leisure** and **pleasure, raucous** and **caucus, fidget** and **digit.**

Guttural. The adjective **guttural,** meaning 'throaty', has a **u** in the second syllable; it has nothing to do with **gutter** and the word **gutteral** does not exist.

Harass. **Harass** and its compounds have only one **r.** (The correct pronunciation of the word is with the stress on the first rather than the second syllable.)

Homogeneous. The accent in this word, which of course means 'uniform in structure and composition', is on the third syllable. A practice exists of spelling it without the second **e** and putting the accent on the second syllable; this may be due to the use of **homogenised** on milk cartons.

Idiosyncrasy, democracy, etc. Like **ecstasy, idiosyncrasy** is spelled with an **s**, and not a **c**, before the **y**, again because of a Greek derivation: it comes from **crasis**, meaning 'mix' (etymologically, an idiosyncrasy is a private cocktail). By contrast, **democracy, aristocracy** and so forth are spelled with a **c** and not an **s** at the end, because they come from **cratos**, meaning 'rule'. **Hypocrisy** is also spelled with **sy** at the end, having nothing to do with rule; **hypocracy** is a somewhat comic mistake.

-ill and -il. Monosyllables rhyming with **hill**, like **fill** and **till**, always end with double **l**; but words with more than one syllable, such as **distil, instil, fulfil** and **until**, normally end with single **l**, even when, as in these examples, the stress is on the last syllable. **Refill** is among the exceptions.

In compounds, the **l** is doubled when followed by a vowel, but not when followed by a consonant: **distillation, fulfilment**.

Inimical. The adjective **inimical**, meaning 'hostile', is so spelled; **inimicable** is probably a confusion with **inimitable**, meaning 'incapable of being imitated'.

Lead and read. Although the past tense and past participle of **to read** are spelled **read**, those of **to lead** are spelled **led**, *not* **lead**, which is the spelling of the name of the metal. Hence **misled** is pronounced with the stress on the second syllable, and is the past tense or past participle of **to mislead**, *not* of a verb **to misle**. (If you remember this last rare but not imaginary mistake, you will never go wrong over the spelling of **led**.)

Mischievous. The word is so spelled and pronounced, not as **mischevious**.

Past and passed. The past tense and past participle of **to pass** is spelled **passed**. **Past** is an adjective applying to time before the present, to things belonging to that time or to the tenses of verbs referring to it. It is also used as a preposition, as in **first past the post**.

Pore. To pore over a book is to study it intently. To misspell **pore** as **pour**, as in **Ministers have been pouring over the text of the treaty**, produces a comic effect.

Possible. The word **possible** is so spelled. The spelling **posable** flouts both principles (5) and (7) at the beginning of this section; if such a word existed, it would probably be pronounced 'pose-able'.

Practice and practise. In Britain, the noun **practice** is spelled with a **c**, the verb **to practise** with an **s**. In the United States, it is the other way round.

Presumptuous. The word is so spelled and pronounced, *not* as **presumptious**; G. M. Hopkins rebuked Robert Bridges for using the latter form, as not being an English word.

Principal and principle. The *adjective*, meaning 'chief', is always

principal. The *noun*, meaning 'rule' or 'theoretical maxim', is **principle**. **Principal** can be used as a noun only when it applies to someone who heads an institution such as a college, a chief party in a contract, one for whom another acts as agent or the amount of a loan or investment apart from the interest.

Programme. This word is spelled in the French manner in Britain and Canada. The spelling **program** was imported from the United States by the agency of the computer business, and should be avoided save in connection with computers.

Publicly. The spelling **publically** has become widespread. The objection that the adjective is not **publical** but **public** does not carry much weight, because the adverbs from **comic** and **tragic** are **comically** and **tragically**. To this it might be replied that **comical** and **tragical** do exist, if only tenuously; but **hedonistical** cannot be claimed to exist, although the adverb is **hedonistically**. It is better simply to say that the word is written, and pronounced, **publicly**.

Separate. This word is so spelled, *not* as **seperate**.

Stationary and *stationery*. **Stationary** is an adjective meaning 're-maining in the same place'. **Stationery** is the collective noun for writing materials, as **cutlery** is the collective noun for eating implements. It is easy to remember which of the pair is which, since *stationery* is stocked by a *stationer*.

Supersede. The verb **to supersede** is often wrongly spelled with a **c**, as **supercede**. This may have originated from a belief that, like **precede**, its second syllable comes from Latin **cedo**, meaning 'yield'; in fact it comes from Latin **sedeo**, meaning 'sit'.

The endings -er, -or and -ar. Words are frequently formed by adding one of these terminations to a verb or, less frequently, a noun, to indicate an agent, i.e. a person or, sometimes, a thing that effects the action in question or produces an object of the kind in question; in the process the final **e** of the original word, if there was one, is dropped, and its final consonant doubled if there is a danger of making a preceding short vowel long. In a very few such words, the ending is **-ar**: **beggar**, **burglar**, **liar**,

pedlar, pulsar, registrar, Templar (note also **scholar**). Otherwise, the ending is usually **-er** unless it is preceded by **t** or **ss**.

There are a number of exceptions: **assignor, author, bailor, conqueror, conveyor, consignor, councillor, counsellor, divisor, donor, error, governor, precursor, purveyor, razor, sailor, sensor, surveyor, survivor, tensor, vendor**; students of law will be able to add a few more. (Note also **censor, stupor, tailor** and **warrior**.) When the word is formed from a verb ending in **-ate**, the termination is almost always **-or**; an exception is **debater** (**eater, heater**, etc., are not, of course, exceptions to *this* rule). After **ss**, the ending is again virtually always **-or**: exceptions are **canvasser** and **trespasser**.

When the termination added to the root word is **-ster**, as in **youngster**, the vowel is always **e**. Otherwise, the ending is usually **-or** after **t**; but there are numerous exceptions – far too many to list here. Most, but by no means all, of them are formed from verbs not derived, directly or through French, from Latin.

The endings -ible and -able. When the word to which the termination **-able** is to be added ends in **ce** or **ge**, the **e** is retained, as in **peaceable**; for **c** and **g** are (as a rule) hard before **a, o** and **u**, and soft before **e** and **i**. Hence unless the **e** were retained before **a**, the **c** or **g** would become hard (**peacable** would be pronounced 'peekable').

There is thus no need to retain the **e** before **-ible**, or to insert one to make a **c** or **g** soft. An **e** is retained *only* in the case just mentioned, and not, for example, in **likable** or **desirable**. The only purpose that an **e** could serve after the **k** or the **r** would be to make the **i** long; and that is redundant, because the general rule is that a vowel is long if it precedes a single consonant followed by another vowel. (**Corrigible** is an exception to *this* rule, but exemplifies the rule that, when followed by **e** or, as here, **i**, **g** is soft.)

Unfortunately, save by appeal to Latin, there is no simple rule for deciding whether the termination should be **-ible** or **-able**: each case has to be learned.

The participial ending -ing. A verb ending in **-ce** or **-ge**, such as **dance, place, rage** or **cringe**, loses the final **e** in the present participle: thus **dancing, placing, raging** and **cringing**. This is because, as stated in the preceding entry, **c** and **g** are soft before **i** (as also before **e**). Two exceptions are **singeing** and **swingeing**, which must be so spelled to distinguish them from **singing** and **swinging**. The participle of a verb ending in **-ng**, such as **singing** and **swinging** themselves, together with **banging**, **ringing**, **winging** and **longing**, is of course an exception to the rule about the soft **g**; you have to know what verb it comes from in order to know how to pronounce it (contrast **hanging** and **ranging**, **winging** and **whinging**). There is for this reason a temptation to retain the **e** in the participle of a verb ending in **-nge**, and write **plungeing**, **lungeing**, etc., but this, though no heinous offence, is nevertheless incorrect.

There is. The frequency of the spelling **their is**, **their could be**, etc. (for **there is**, **there could be**) in Final Examination papers is probably due to slips of the pen; but it has prompted me to insert this item.

The terminations -ent and -ant. There is no exceptionless rule, but the tendency is for adjectives to end in **-ent** and for nouns to end in **-ant**: thus **is dependent on** but **provide for her dependants**. However, **existent** is both an adjective and a noun. When the termination **-ent** is possible, the abstract noun usually ends in **-ence** (**existence**, **dependence**); contrast **accordance**.

The termination -gue. Although English contains words like **dog** and **hog**, many words ending with a hard **g** sound follow French in adding silent **-ue** at the end: examples are **catalogue** and **dialogue** (note also **harangue**). Americans often omit the final **-ue**, no doubt for fear it will be pronounced, as it is in **ague** and **argue**; but they are not consistent, writing **Ivy League** rather than **Ivy Leag**. The **-ue** should be retained by Cisatlantic writers.

To, two and too. It is sad to have to say it, but there are three words all spelled differently: the preposition **to** (with short vowel); the number-word **two** (with long vowel); and the adverb **too** (also with long vowel), meaning 'excessively' or 'also'.

Tortuous. The adjective **tortuous** meaning, literally or metaphorically, 'twisting and turning', 'devious', is so spelled, *not* as **torturous**; it has nothing, save etymologically, to do with **torture**.

Unequivocally. The adjectives are **equivocal** and **unequivocal**, and the adverbs **equivocally** and **unequivocally**. **Unequivocably** and its kindred are solecisms. The terminations **-able** and **-ably** always connote capacity.

-y. Words ending in **y** change the **y** to **ie** when inflected by the addition of **-s** for the plural or third person singular: thus **bully/bullies; belly/bellies; spy/spies; deny/denies**. When **-ing** is added, the **y** is retained, as in **trying** and **bullying**; indeed, final **-ie** becomes **y**, e.g. **die/dying, lie/lying**. When **-er, -est, -ness** or **-ly** is added, final **y** is normally changed to **i**: thus **supply/supplier; carry/carrier; dry/drier, drily; happy/happier, happiness, happily; tidy/tidier, tidiness, tidily**. The *Concise Oxford Dictionary* prefers **shyly** to **shily**, however. **Shyness, shyer, dryness** and **scryer** (from the verb **to scry**) are unquestionably correct.

It is sometimes argued that it is unnecessary nowadays to know how to spell, since, if one uses a word processor, one can activate the spelling checker. Apart from the fact that most spelling checkers give American spellings, which a poor speller will be unable to recognise, there is also the disadvantage that it will fail to detect mistakes like **weather** for **whether, hire** for **higher, insure** for **ensure** and **stationery** for **stationary**. Moreover, with spellings as bad as some encountered in examination scripts, the checker will either offer no suggestions at all or a great number, between which an incompetent speller will not know how to choose; I have verified this by running lists of such errors through my own spelling checker. Besides, a spelling checker is not always available, for instance during an examination.

7. Ideological and Other Usages

Gender and sex. This point and the next two have been left nearly until last, as being the only ones involving ideology. The word **gender** used to be applied exclusively to nouns, pronouns and adjectives in Indo-European and Semitic languages to indicate the distinction between masculine and feminine, or masculine, feminine and neuter; one of the uses of the word **sex** was to distinguish between male and female human beings and animals. (The 1969 edition of *The American Heritage Dictionary* recognises only the grammatical use of **gender**.)

Anthropologists borrowed the word **gender** from the grammarians in order to distinguish social from biological classification: a transvestite might be of the female gender, though of the male sex. For a reason obscure to me, feminists have recently promoted the use of **gender** as a substitute for the word **sex** in the use mentioned above, even when the distinction is purely biological; they still, however, speak of **sexism** and not of **genderism**.

The change seems pointless, and is surely to be deprecated: it makes it impossible, or at least clumsy, for example, to explain that in English the gender of the third-person pronoun depends on the sex of the person referred to, but, in German, on the gender of the preceding noun. It also ruins the immortal line spoken by Jack Lemmon in *Some Like it Hot*, 'It's a whole different sex'.

He, she, they. Until quite recently, **he** has been the pronoun of common gender in sentences like **If anyone were to come in now, he would be very surprised, she** being used only when there was a presumption that a person of the kind in question would be a woman. Now, for some time, there has been a feminist campaign against this use of **he**.

The charge is not that it was intended to confine the application to men: if it were, it would be quite mistaken. **"Who can point out the road to his own felicity?"**, Fanny Burney's Cecilia asks herself, generalising from her own case; she unselfconsciously uses **his** as of common gender, since to use **her** would have confined the application to women. The charge is, rather, that the use constitutes subliminal propaganda for the view that women are deviations from the human norm.

I am highly sceptical that it had any such effect: it is not noticeable that male speakers of languages like Latin, Greek, German and Malay possessing a single word for 'human being' not connoting maleness in any context have been any less sexist than speakers of those, like English and French, lacking such a word. The campaign against the **he** of common gender nevertheless makes it difficult so to use **he** without selfconsciousness. Many people are sufficiently impressed by the propaganda to wish to avoid that use: the problem is to find an alternative.

The form s/he is unpronounceable as well as hideous. The use of **he or she** is tolerable occasionally, but not repeatedly in a single sentence or even paragraph. Virtually all American academics (surely not other Americans) have gone over to using **she** as of common gender in such sentences as **If a sceptic were asked this question, she would reply ....** They do this even when there is a strong presumption that the person would be male, often with ludicrous results, as in **If an Athenian general had been asked this question, she would have replied ....**

If, after a century or two, this use of **she** comes to seem natural, while the use of **he** appears to confine the application to males, I do not see that anything will have been gained. In the meantime, the use appears ridiculous to many readers, or at least makes them hesitate each time to check whether women had been particularly referred to.

A solution adopted by some is to use **they** with a singular sense, on the ground that this is indeed often done in colloquial speech. In writing, however, it can lead to ambiguities, as in **When a reporter questions the rebels, their credentials are not enquired after.** (Ambiguous sentences of this kind have not infrequently appeared in newspapers.) It is better, when writing, to preserve the grammatical principle that **they** is a plural pronoun. Often this can be done by simply making the subject plural. **A sceptic never abandons their principles** sounds horrible, and is quite unnecessary: exactly the same thought can be expressed by **Sceptics never abandon their principles.** When this remedy is inapplicable, as to **If someone suffers from loss of memory, they become a different person**, a construction with a relative clause will often serve: **Someone who suffers from loss of memory becomes a different person.**

It is indeed a good rule to avoid giving unnecessary offence to readers. Since some readers will be offended by the **he** of common gender, it is worth avoiding its use when periphrasis will allow the thought to be otherwise expressed without clumsiness. Occasionally this cannot be done, however: in the absence of any reasonable alternative, it is then best to use **he** as it was always formerly used.

There is, of course, no excuse for using **they** when referring to a specific individual of determinate sex, as in the sentence **I do not think that an objective reader of the full transcript ... could conclude other than the Department's witness did their utmost to assist the court** (from a letter to the *Guardian* by Lord Brabazon of Tara on 10 January 1992): the reference was to a particular male official witness at the Lockerbie inquiry, already referred to in the letter as **he**.

The sentence contains three mistakes in seven words: it should read ... **could conclude otherwise than that the Department's witness did his utmost ...** (see 2(b) under *Other*, and, concerning **that**, 2(e)). It seems that Ministers of the Crown and their civil servants could also benefit from a refresher course in English grammar.

Man, men. The word **man**, as a generic word for 'human being' and as denoting the human race, is under severe attack from the feminist camp. It is a minor misfortune of English to have no word for these purposes distinct from the word opposed to **woman** and meaning 'male human being' (usually 'male human adult', but not in the phrase **man child**); but until very recently English speakers have managed without discomfort with a dual use of a single word. That, the feminists would have us think, has resulted in a psychological conditioning to believe in the superiority of the male sex.

The case is not parallel to the discouragement of the formerly prevalent use of the word **native** as applying to all those with skins of hue darker than white, and only to them, regardless of whether they were living in the country of their birth. Not only did that involve a *misuse* of a word with a clear meaning, but it ineluctably conveyed a contemptuous, or at best patronising, attitude founded upon a racist ideology. It cannot be said that contempt was expressed either by the word **woman** or by the use of **man** as embracing both sexes; at worst, the propaganda was subliminal.

Everyone who writes in English is forced to take sides on this issue, however much he might wish to avoid it. In favour of not using **man** in the way objected to is the feminist argument: can we be sure that, in so using it, we are not expressing, or making subliminal propaganda for, an assumption of male superiority? There is also the fact that, whether or not the feminist case is sound, the use offends those who have accepted that case.

Feminists ought for their part to acknowledge that there is much to set against the change. There is, first, the fact that no adequate substitute has been proposed. Secondly, there is the retrospective effect that such a change would have upon familiar phrases like **man and beast, God and man** and **the children of men,** and on countless passages from English literature and the liturgy. This is not the *same* point: if we had an adequate replacement for **man** in the sense objected to, we could use it from now on; but that would not restore our ability to read such passages as they were meant. Here is a selection of passages in which **man** in the singular is so used: **Man proposes, God disposes** (Thomas à Kempis in translation); **What a piece of work is man!** (*Hamlet*); **and was made man** (the Nicene Creed); **The Descent of Man** (Darwin); **The proper study of mankind is man** (Pope); **the Sabbath is made for man, not man for the Sabbath** (*St Mark*); **Put not your trust in princes, nor in any child of man** (*Psalms*); **To justify God's ways to man** (Housman); **God made man in his own image; … male and female he created them** (*Genesis*); **Of man's first disobedience** (Milton). Hamlet, having said **Man delights not me**, obviously using **man** in the sense under discussion, plays upon the other sense by adding **No, nor woman neither, though by your smiling you seem to say so.** And here is a selection of passages in which **men,** in the plural, is used as applying to both sexes: **To justify the ways of God to men** (Milton); **more than men believe** (Chesterton); **for us men, and for our salvation** (the Nicene Creed); **the tongues of men and of angels** (*1 Corinthians*); **the tired men and dogs all gone to rest** (Matthew Arnold); **no other name under heaven given to men, whereby we must be saved** (*Acts*).

If the collective use of the word **man** comes to denote the male sex rather than the human race, and its use as count-noun to apply exclusively to male human beings, a generation will grow up ignorant that it had any other use; its members will then misinterpret passages like those cited and, no doubt, will be accordingly shocked. We have to decide whether the feminist case is so strong as to outweigh the damage done to the understanding of the literature of the past and of formulas still in use for which no sensible or dignified replacement has been proposed; for, to repeat, their authors had no intention of promoting any belief in male superiority, and were in no way meaning to use **man** or **men,** in such contexts, with a connotation of maleness. It is each individual's choice how he comes down on this issue, though the choices made will affect us all. All I can do is to offer a personal opinion; and my opinion is that the feminists' case in not nearly strong enough to justify the price they ask us to pay. The pair **man/woman** is not unique in its asymmetry. That is shared by **horse/mare**, **dog/bitch**, **goose/gander**, **duck/drake** and many others. It is difficult to believe that these asymmetries make subliminal propaganda for the idea that, among horses and dogs, females represent a deviation from the norm, but that, among geese and ducks, it is males that do. It is difficult to believe that anyone has any such absurd idea: we are merely dealing with a quirk of language. Nor, as already remarked, is the idea of male superiority less strong among, say, Germans, who speak one of the several languages in which there is one word for 'human being' in general, and a distinct one for 'male human being'. (The proof that there was no intention, in the Biblical and liturgical passages cited, to confine the application to males is that they are translations from such languages.) These facts do not disprove the contention that our usage promotes a belief in male superiority; but they show that the alleged effect cannot be demonstrated from the mere existence of the usage, but requires more evidence. The feminist case is not based on recognisable fact, but on speculation; far firmer grounds are needed before we should think of inflicting such damage on what has come down to us from the past.

*

I conclude with three changes in the language over the last thirty years that involve no points of style or grammar and bear little on examination answers.

Corn. One victim of American impact on our usage is the word **corn**, which used to be one of the most evocative in the language. Until long after the Second World War, it was a generic term for wheat, barley, oats and rye, and, with that meaning, figured in many loved and lovely phrases from poetry, anthems, hymns and the Bible: **when, sick for home, she stood in tears amid the alien corn** (Keats); **the valleys smile with waving corn; Fair waved the golden corn; the valleys also shall stand so thick with corn, that they shall laugh and sing** (Psalms, Book of Common Prayer). Titles have been drawn from these: Somerset Maugham's *The Alien Corn*; Samuel Palmer's *The Valley Thick with Corn*. Under American influence, the word has now been largely appropriated for what was formerly called maize or Indian corn. This is a mild impoverishment of the language, depriving it of the generic term; but it is chiefly to be deplored for rendering unintelligible or ludicrous a great number of phrases, such as those quoted above, from poetry and elsewhere: this may be termed retroactive linguistic destruction.

The change is not yet definitive: neither the traditional use of the word **corn** nor the term **Indian corn** is wholly obsolete. It is therefore worth striving to reinstate the former sense of **corn**, both by using it in that sense whenever it obviously could not mean 'maize', and by using **maize** or **Indian corn** whenever referring to that very untypical cereal.

Billion, trillion. The next two changes are even more recent. **Billion** and **trillion** are rare examples of words whose meanings were changed by the deliberate effort of outsiders, without the bulk of the native population's noticing that a change had taken place. In United States usage, **billion** has always meant a thousand million (1,000,000,000). In British usage up to the 1970s, it meant a million million (1,000,000,000,000).

Likewise, in the United States **trillion** means a million million, whereas in former British usage it meant a million million million. Since the prefix **bi-** means 'two' (as in **bicentennial, bicycle,** etc.), and the prefix **tri-** similarly means 'three', the British usage was obviously more reasonable, given that a million million is the square of a million, and a million million million the cube of a million, whereas a thousand million is not the square of any whole number, and a million million is, irrelevantly, the cube of ten thousand.

The change to the American usage was effected here in a particular year in the 1970s (I now forget which), mainly through the medium of television, on which there coincided a popular series of lectures on cosmology by Carl Sagan and numerous appearances by American economists. Sagan announced aggressively that, while he knew that it did not have that meaning here, he would use the word **billion** in its American sense; all the economists used the word in the same sense, without notification.

They may or may not have known that they were courting misunderstanding; even if not, they plainly would not have cared if they had been told. Many British broadcasters, especially on economic subjects, copied their example, though some continued to say **a thousand million**. The assault was quite wanton, since there was already in the language a word, admittedly seldom used, meaning 'a thousand million', namely **milliard**. The result was a confused period of about two years, during which it was difficult to be sure what anyone meant by the word **billion**; in the whole of this time, hardly anybody evinced any awareness of a shift or uncertainty of meaning.

At the end of the period, **billion** and **trillion** were firmly installed in their American senses; **America's Savings and Loan scandal could cost taxpayers somewhere between a few hundred billion and a trillion dollars** (*Independent*, 20 July 1991) shows that reference to the larger number is sometimes needed. It is certainly fruitless now to use **billion** without explanation in its old sense of a million million, and there must be many unaware that it ever had that sense, let alone that it had it until so very recently; but, if one wishes, as a victim of this minor piece of cultural rape, to retain what dignity one can, one may say **a thousand million** and **a million million** (or even **10 to the 9th** and **10 to the 12th**), eschewing **billion** and **trillion** altogether.

Pee. This word acquired a new meaning with the introduction of decimal currency. During the period when both the old and the new currencies were in use, the smallest units in each were distinguished by the abbreviations **d.** and **p.** respectively; this naturally led to people's speaking of **five pee** rather than **five new pence**. Now that the old currency has long been gone, **pee** has remained.

The word is childish: it is surely time to revive the old word **penny** with its two plurals **pennies** (for the coins) and **pence** (for sums of money), and the contractions **tuppence**, **threepence**, etc. It would be a pity if proverbs like **Look after the pence, and the pounds will look after themselves** and **In for a penny, in for a pound** were to become incomprehensible.

Conclusion

The objection may be raised to this book that it attempts to impose rules that held for the English of fifty years ago, but do not hold for the English of today: the language has irrevocably changed. The answer is that the changes in question are *not* irrevocable. They are all changes that are not yet definitively established, and that continue to offend many people, whereas the older forms, while far less often observed than they used to be, do not yet offend anybody or strike anybody as awkward or antiquated. On the contrary, many people, reading prose written in conformity to them, find it exceptionally clear or pleasing, without being able to analyse why it makes this impression on them. Furthermore, this book has attempted to show, in most of these cases, why the changes are for the worse, and weaken the expressive power of the language.

Suppose that someone who accepted that the grammatical rules of English have irrevocably changed were to try to write a guide like this (say to help foreign students): what would it look like? Well, the grammatical rules it laid down would be enormously more complicated that those stated here. Consider, for instance, what it would have to say about the forms **I** and **me**. It could not say that the two were interchangeable: for no one would say **Me am going** or **Me is going**, while **He hit I** is unarguably a dialect form, not usable by anyone with no right to that dialect. But it could not give the traditional rule that **I** is to be used in subject position, and **me** in object position or after a preposition, because 'modern' usage admits **Me and him are going**, at least in the spoken language, and **It will not affect you and I** in the written language also. It would have, therefore, to lay down the rule that, when the pronoun stands alone, the form is **I** in subject position, and **me** in other positions, but that when it is part of a compound phrase, with a noun or other pronoun joined to it by **and**, the rule is reversed. Likewise with **he** and **him**: it would have to say that **him** is used as object or after a preposition, save when preceding a relative pronoun, as in **to he who** … These rules are far more complex than those given in this book, and hard for a foreigner, or a child, to learn.

To this it may be answered that grammatical rules are imposed in order to distinguish a supposed social élite from the rest. The assumption is that this elitist practice used to prevail, but has now been superseded. The precise reverse holds good. Fifty years ago, *all* schools taught correct grammar and spelling, and how to write so as to make one's meaning plain: those who went to State schools, even if they left quite early, could therefore learn how to write as good English as anyone else. Now the public schools continue to teach these things, while many teachers at State schools imbue their pupils with the idea that rules of grammar and principles of style have no authority and should be scorned as 'elitist': they thereby promote much *greater* differentiation and hence inequality than before.

It may still be stubbornly maintained that grammatical rules do not matter, and in effect do not exist. We can ignore them and speak in any manner we like, provided that we convey what we mean, because there is no such thing as correct speech or writing: whatever is said or written is thereby correct, because there is no external standard of correctness. This is a half-truth: being able to convey what one means depends upon the general acceptance of rules determining correct forms of expression. Certainly you can often convey your meaning despite having expressed yourself incorrectly, because the hearer realises that you could not be meaning what you have actually said, and can guess what you intended. If enough people make the mistake you made, it will indeed cease to be a mistake: this is one way in which a language changes. It does not follow that there *are* no grammatical rules now. On the contrary, everyone obeys some grammatical rules or other: the question is which deserve our obedience.

Consider a foreigner learning English. If his teacher lets him think that **I** and **me** are interchangeable, he *will* say things like **Me will meet you at the café**; and he will be regarded with amusement for betraying his inadequate command of the language, since no native speaker says that. If the teacher wishes this not to happen to his pupil, he *must* tell him that you cannot say **Me will**, **Me am** or **Me is**. Someone who knows English well will avoid saying such things, even if he believes that he does not obey any grammatical rules, because he knows that saying them would invite mockery: he wants to speak as others do. In avoiding them, he *is* obeying a grammatical rule; to speak as others do, one must obey the same grammatical rules as they. There cannot be a language without grammatical rules.

No one should think, 'I am an English speaker, and therefore *make* the language: hence I am not bound by the rules of English grammar'. When you learn French, you accept that you are bound by the rules of French grammar; how long do you suppose that you have to have been speaking French, or how well do you suppose that you have to speak it, before you cease to be bound by them? It is true that you have power, in the sense that, if you flout a rule, and induce sufficiently many others to flout it, it will no longer be a rule: you and the others will have changed the language. But, precisely because your power over the rules is greater, you bear *greater* responsibility than towards rules your violation of which will not affect their remaining in force.

Grammatical rules help to make intended meaning clear. Colloquial speech differs greatly in this regard from writing. In speech, intonation, gestures and facial expressions all help to make the speaker's meaning apparent; if it is not apparent, he may be asked to explain. Moreover, the sentences are usually shorter and less complex than those appropriate in writing. If there is an accepted standard of grammatical propriety in the written language, a writer will be able to rely on this to distinguish his meaning from a different one his sentence could not bear, if grammatically correct.

Often, in the simpler sentences used in speech, a grammatical mistake will not impair the hearer's understanding: but, if this mistake becomes common in the written language, the grammatical rule will no longer be able to distinguish between one meaning and another, and, if you show yourself indifferent to correct grammar, *you* will be unable to make your meaning plain without unwieldy periphrasis. One who respects grammar may still be able to do so, just because he is known to respect it; but, if grammatical rules are widely neglected, no one will be able to count on his readers' expecting them to be obeyed. Neglecting grammatical rules may thus very well impoverish the expressive power of the language.

To say that it does not matter whether you flout the rules as long as you convey your meaning is like saying that it does not matter that you are using a finely ground razor to cut the string, as long as the string is cut. *You* may convey your meaning on that occasion: you risk making it harder for others to express theirs, or for you to do so on a later occasion. The effect may last for generations to come, or perhaps in perpetuity: the language will have been permanently impaired. Existing human languages are instruments far more finely tuned and far more complex than any machine: damaging them by misuse is more heinous a crime than wrecking an expensive machine.

Not all linguistic changes are by any means for the better. If you use an expression or a grammatical construction in a sense which it has not previously borne, and your mistake is widely copied, you will have made it difficult for anyone subsequently to use it in its original sense, for fear of being misunderstood; and if there was already a perfectly good way of expressing what you used it to express, you will have impoverished the language, without any compensating advantage.

We did not invent our mother-tongue, any more than any other language that we have learned: we inherited it. It was created over centuries by generations of our forebears; and most of them, whether well or poorly educated, literate or illiterate, treated it with respect. All languages are the co-operative creations of human beings; they are marvellous instruments for the expression and communication of thought and feeling, and vehicles for private thought. Each generation makes changes in them, but all have the responsibility for handing them on to the next generation in at least as perfect a condition as that in which they themselves inherited them. Disrespect for one's language is ingratitude to our forebears and selfishness towards our descendants.

Molluscs from a polluted sea such as the Mediterranean are dangerous to eat, because they absorb and concentrate in their bodies all the poisons floating in the waters. Many people are linguistic molluscs. A vogue word or piece of jargon, a misspelling or grammatical mistake, has only to appear once in a newspaper for them eagerly to adopt it, even though they have hitherto been spelling the word correctly or observing the grammatical rule all their lives; a linguistic Gresham's law, more potent today than ever before, is thus enforced. Do not be a linguistic mollusc.

The way to avoid being one is to cultivate the habit of being conscious, as you read and as you listen to others, as you write and, if possible, as you speak, of the forms of expression used as well as of their content. Doing so will enable you to spot some opportunities for jokes, too, which you would otherwise have missed.

This book is not 'elitist'; to think it is is to react in accordance with a conditioned reflex. The book has no restricted circulation; it is not written for an élite, but for anybody who wishes to make use of it. Admittedly, it was composed with examination candidates particularly in mind; but it is available to all, and its author greatly hopes that many who wish to improve the way they write will find it of help to them. Doubtless all readers will find something they disagree with; even if they are right, and I in error, they will have been prompted to give greater conscious thought to our shared language, a habit few are nowadays encouraged to acquire.

Final Exercises

Now that you have read (or at least skimmed) this book, go back to the preliminary test at the end of the introductory section, and see if you can spot any mistakes that you missed when you first looked at it.

Here is the paragraph again, with references to the mistakes noted in this book:

Neither capitalism nor socialism are (1) capable of diffusing (2) this problem; and neither (3) is it desireable (4) that either solution is (5) attempted. We should not loose (6) this opportunity to not only (7) devise a new type of system but to (8) at the same time (7) manage our affairs such (9) that we remain within the broad parameters (10) defined by our democratic tradition. Having said this, (11) it is important to take on board (10) the fact that unequivocably (12) disasterous (13) consequences will result from us trying (14) to run before we can walk (10). Those sort of (15) consequences have already lead (16) to unrest and conflict in the majority (17) of the continent; we can only (18) escape them if we forego (19) our habitual inclination to act in haste and repent at leasure (20). The above quote (21) from the German Chancellor, and it's (22) stern words of warning, exemplifies (1) some of the best thinking about these matters that are (1) taking place at this moment in time (10); that is why it has had such positive feedback (23). We ought to better (7) appreciate that opportunities seldom present themselves other (24) than briefly to whomever (25) can take advantage of them; for he who (26) would not be left adrift in the ongoing (27) march of events (28), there is no other alternative (29) but to seek a middle path between one calamity laden (30) socio-economic mechanism (28) and the other. We must put to ourselves the question as to (31) whether to seek it, or, alternately (29), to ever sink (7) deeper into stagnation in terms of (32) our economy.

See:

(1) 2(g)
(2) *Defuse and diffuse* in 5
(3) *And nor, but nor, and neither* in 2(e)
(4) *The endings -ible and -able* in 6
(5) 2(j)
(6) *Lose and loose* in 5
(7) *Split infinitives* in 3
(8) *Either ... or; both ... and; not only ... but also* in 2(e)
(9) *Such, so* in 2(b)
(10) *Clichés* in 3
(11) *Dangling participles* in 2(d)
(12) *Unequivocally* in 6
(13) *Disastrous* in 6
(14) 2(d)
(15) *Sort of* in 2(g)
(16) *Lead and read* in 6
(17) *Majority* in 2(h)
(18) *Only* in 3
(19) *For- and fore-* in 6
(20) *Fraternal twins* in 6
(21) *Quote* in 3
(22) APOSTROPHES in 4
(23) *Feedback* in 5
(24) *Other* in 2(b)
(25) *Whoever and whomever* in 2(a)
(26) *He who* in 2(a)
(27) *Ongoing* in 3
(28) *Mixed metaphors* in 3
(29) *Alternative(ly) and alternate(ly)* in 5
(30) HYPHENS in 4

EXERCISE 2

Here is a short passage from *The Plant Report: a working party on Electoral Reform* (1991):

> If some explicitly proportional system were to be introduced for institutions other than the House of Commons which was to retain a plurality system of election, then there is a danger, perhaps most acute with the Second Chamber, that if it were to be elected on a proportional basis that it could claim greater legitimacy in some constitutional deadlock with the Commons. This could be mitigated to a great extent if the Commons itself were to be elected on a majoritarian basis following an exhaustive ballot which the Alternative Vote is although, as it were, telescoped into a single act of voting. It might be the case that given there are the two sorts of ideas of legitimacy at work in society: a proportional one and a majoritarian one that dead-

lock could be avoided if one of these the majoritarian one was in fact absolutely so rather than relatively so under First Past the Post.

We often talk like this; it will not pass muster to *write* like this. Try rewriting this passage clearly and grammatically, before looking at the comments that follow.

COMMENTS

It was already pointed out, in 2(e), that, in the first sentence, grammar requires the conjunction **that** to occur only once. Looking at the whole sentence, however, we realise that the conditional clause occurs twice, quite unnecessarily, in slightly different words, and that the relative clause ought properly to be part of it.

Further, the writer seems to forget, towards the end of the sentence, that he started out to talk of *any* other political institution (a Scottish Assembly, for example), and not just of the Second Chamber; the pronoun **it** fails to refer back to the plural phrase **institutions other than the House of Commons.**

This first sentence may thus be emended as follows:

If the House of Commons were to retain a plurality system of election, but some other political institution – above all, the Second Chamber – were to be elected on a proportional basis, there would be a danger of its claiming greater legitimacy in some constitutional deadlock with the Commons.

What principally renders the second sentence confusing is the clumsiness of the clause **which the Alternative Vote is**; the reader's difficulty is exacerbated by the virtual absence of commas. Having saved some words in the first sentence, we can afford to expand somewhat for the sake of clarity:

This might be greatly mitigated if the Commons were to be elected on a majoritarian rather than a plurality basis, by means of an exhaustive ballot method; though telescoped into a single act of voting, the Alternative Vote system may rank as such a method.

The third sentence is perhaps the worst. If the second occurrence of **that** is meant as a conjunction, it embodies the same mistake as in the first sentence: only one **that** is needed. It may be intended as a demonstrative adjective, however, referring to the deadlock previously mentioned; if so, ambiguity could have been avoided by using **such a deadlock** in place of **that deadlock**.

The final phrase **under First Past the Post** requires **as** in front of it; but it is the double occurrence of **so** that may perplex the reader. For what word or phrase is it meant to stand proxy? The writer has referred to *two* ideas or principles (**sorts of** is quite redundant), the proportional and the majoritarian. He then recommends adopting one of them in an absolute rather than a relative form, specifying which, namely the majoritarian principle. He is here contrasting appeal to an absolute majority with appeal to a relative majority or plurality; but the sentence is written so as to suggest that there are also absolute and relative versions of proportionality, which, of course, he does not mean. The absence of any punctuation other than the colon again exacerbates the syntactical confusion. The form of expression is very slack; the question is not whether the majoritarian principle *is* absolutely or relatively majoritarian, but whether it is adopted in one or other form. The word **given** registers that it is not really necessary to *say* in this sentence that there are these two principles: that has been repeatedly emphasised throughout the *Report*, but the writer has found no way to avoid saying it yet again. An emended version might run:

> **Such a deadlock might be less of a threat if, of the two competing principles, proportional and majoritarian, the latter were adopted in the strict form, requiring an absolute majority and not merely a relative one as under First Past the Post.**

EXERCISE 3

The circumstance that has compelled me to draw many of my examples from newspapers may give the false impression that I regard journalists, as a class, as uniquely bad writers. By examining two paragraphs from official Oxford University documents I may to some degree correct this impression. One is from the minutes of a meeting of the Board of the Faculty of English Language and Literature, the other from a communication to faculty boards by a committee of the General Board.

One item of the minutes ran as follows:

**Report of the Working Party on the Centre for the Study
of the Performing Arts**

**The board received the report of the working party and warmly
welcomed the initiative to establish a Centre for the Study of
the Performing Arts, on the basis that it would be established
and supported entirely on external funding. It took the view that
the centre would be an extremely valuable resource for a number of current faculty members and for the increasing cohort
of graduate students already involved in theatre-related research; and might well be of interest also to the Murdoch
Professor. It was *agreed* that the board should give further
consideration to its policy on media and performance-related
initiative, probably when the appointment to the Murdoch
chair had been made.**

This paragraph, with very slight changes, was forwarded by the Faculty
Board to the General Board, the last sentence then beginning:

**The Board intends to give further consideration to the area of
media and performance-related initiatives, ...**

In this short paragraph, we have *two* adjectives formed by adding
-related to a noun; some vogue words (**resource, cohort** and **initiative**,
the second occurrence of which is quite meaningless); and repeated slack
phrases in constant use by bureaucrats (**on the basis that, took the view,
involved in, give further consideration to, the area of**). Reading this
document would hardly encourage anyone ambitious to become a writer
to study English at Oxford.

Section 10 of the committee's letter to all faculty boards runs as
follows:

**One question not referred to the committee by Council or the
General Board is that of the interplay between current syllabus
arrangements and the load on academic staff. The committee
wishes to know whether it is the case that proliferation of
options leads to undesirable fragmentation of teaching effort
and consequent artificial overload on members of the academic
staff. Faculty boards are *asked to consider* (where they are not**

already doing so) whether syllabus arrangements might be adjusted to reduce the overall load on academic staff: and what it would be necessary to do from the point of view of the syllabus (if the current equilibrium of duties and payments were to remain intact) in order to free academic staff to provide them with more time to do research. The committee also *seeks details* of the apparatus which faculty boards already have in place to monitor and control the effect of syllabus structures on teaching load.

Setting aside the use of **staff** as a plural noun, eschewed in the second sentence but explicit at the end of the third, one's first thought might be that a *question* is better specified by a clause than by a noun-phrase starting **that of**; so the first sentence might be amended to:

One question not referred to the committee by Council or the General Board is what interplay there is between current syllabus arrangements and the load on academic staff.

For myself, I do not greatly care for **interplay** when no play of any kind is at issue; **interaction** lacks the inappropriate suggestion, and allows us to substitute a verb for one of the countless abstract nouns. We thus obtain:

One question not referred to the committee by Council or the General Board is how current syllabus arrangements interact with the load on academic staff.

Now both **interplay** and **interact** lead us to expect a discussion of the effects of each item on the other. The remaining three sentences, however, speak only of the effect of syllabus options on teaching load; that of teaching load on syllabus options is simply not canvassed. **Interplay** and **interact** are therefore misleading; we need something like:

One question not referred to the committee by Council or the General Board is whether current syllabus arrangements increase the load on academic staff.

The first two sentences are now beginning to look repetitive; perhaps they might be run together. Certainly **it is the case that** can be excised from the second without loss; it contributes nothing whatever. Further, **artificial** seems the wrong word; **avoidable** or **unnecessary** would surely be better. When we run the two sentences together, do we need to inform readers that the question the committee is asking was not suggested by Council or the General Board? If not, we can have:

> **The committee wishes to know whether the proliferation of syllabus options fragments teaching effort and so increases teaching load unnecessarily.**

If Council and the General Board must be mentioned, this can be expanded to:

> **The committee, in this instance unprompted by Council and the General Board, wishes to know whether the proliferation of syllabus options fragments teaching effort and so increases teaching load unnecessarily.**

But such a first sentence is as bad an introduction to the two that follow as was the committee's second sentence. It says it **wishes to know** the answer to a question, but assumes in the rest of the section that the answer is **Yes**. As a final version, therefore, we must put:

> **The committee suspects that the proliferation of syllabus options fragments teaching effort and so increases teaching load unnecessarily.**

Eighteen words in place of fifty-nine, and, save for omitting the reference to Council and the General Board, saying no less and saying it more accurately.

Now for the remaining two sentences. In the first half of the third sentence, the parenthesis seems redundant: those faculty boards already considering the matter are not being asked to stop considering it. The word **overall** is also redundant, since not contrasted with anything: the committee is not suggesting increasing one part of the load so as to achieve an overall (or net) reduction. Finally, the word **arrangements** is superfluous: no contrast is intended between an adjustment of the *syllabus* and an adjustment of the *arrangements* governing it. We thus obtain:

Faculty boards are *asked to consider* **whether the syllabus might be revised so as to reduce the load on those who teach it:**

The second half of the sentence contains the phrase **in order to free academic staff to provide them with more time to do research**. The construction **in order to do X to do Y**, when the second **to** has the sense of 'in order to', is extremely awkward. Moreover, it is quite unnecessary here, because the staff are not being freed in any other way than by being given more time to do research; so **in order to provide academic staff with more time to do research** conveys the same sense, and has the additional advantage of not explicitly treating **staff** as plural. The sentence also contains the slipshod phrase **what it would be necessary to do from the point of view of the syllabus**. A syllabus does not have a point of view; what is meant is **to do to the syllabus**. Again, we have a largely redundant parenthesis. At the most, **under present arrangements** would meet the case; but it surely is not necessary at all. In any case, the entire second half of the sentence merely repeats, more vaguely, what was said in the first half, since the committee is obviously not envisaging doing anything 'from the point of view of the syllabus' save to reduce the number of options; the only new element is the specification of the reason for reducing the teaching load. The third sentence may therefore simply read:

Faculty boards are *asked to consider* **whether the syllabus might be revised so as to reduce the load on those who teach it, in order to give them more time for research**.

Thirty-two words in place of seventy, this time.

The final sentence is very menacing. If the effect was intentional, it was a breach of manners rather than a fault of style; but, when the style is bad, it is difficult to be sure of the intention. If the menace was unintended, it would be removed by rephrasing the sentence as:

If any faculty boards have been seeking to stop teaching loads from becoming too heavy by monitoring the effect of their syllabuses upon them, the committee *wishes to be told the details*.

This time the number of words has increased from twenty-seven to thirty-two: politeness is usually the enemy of abruptness. In all, the emendations made here have reduced a hundred and fifty-six words to eighty-two. Their aim was not condensation, but an improvement of style; but stylistic inelegance of the type found in official documents frequently results in wordiness. An effort to reform their style would save paper and the recipients' reading time.

EXERCISE 4

On 22 June 1991, the *Spectator* printed a letter of which the main paragraph is reproduced below, offering a prize to the first reader to identify all the mistakes in it. The letter was addressed to a constituent by a prominent MP, whom it would be unfair to name, since comparable letters have no doubt been written by many MPs. As a fourth test, see how many mistakes you can spot (most but not all of them have been listed in this book).

> **I believe that the one single most significant change that we could take in Britain in the next ten years would be to change our political and electoral system. Decentralise government and return power to each individual elector. One of the most extraordinary anomalies arising from the prominantly disasterous situation the government has got themselves into over the poll tax is, that where we could have had two years ago a government elected by proportional representation there is one thing that is certain that the government would never have been allowed introduce the poll tax. Government's over the years have to take difficult decisions, decisions that sometimes require sacrifices by significant proportions of the electorate. The chance of obtaining majority acceptance of these decisions are much more likely when they arise from the views of the consensus of the whole of the British people.**

Now rewrite the paragraph in decent English.

Index

Words that occur as the first word of a heading in Section 5 or 6 are not included in the index.